The Anthropology of Landscape: A Guide to Neolithic Sites in Cardiganshire, Carmarthenshire & Pembrokeshire

Monuments in the Landscape

Volume V

The Anthropology of Landscape: A Guide to Neolithic Sites in Cardiganshire, Carmarthenshire & Pembrokeshire

by
George Children and George Nash

Logaston Press

LOGASTON PRESS
Little Logaston Woonton Almeley
Herefordshire HR3 6QH

First published by Logaston Press 1997
Revised edition published 2002
Copyright © George Children and George Nash 1997 & 2002

ISBN 1 873827 99 7

Set in Times by Logaston Press
and printed in Great Britain by
Bell & Bain Ltd, Glasgow

To Richard and George Edward

Please Note

Some of the monuments mentioned in this book are situated on private land and permission from the owner must, therefore, be obtained before visiting them. The owner's residence is given for those sites detailed in the guide section.

All the sites covered in this book date from the Neolithic period. No metal objects are present on sites of this date. In the case of Neolithic stray finds, only four-figure grid references have been used.

The following points must be observed:

1. Always follow the Countryside Code.

2. On all sites, extreme care should be taken.

3. Any artefacts found on sites in south-west Wales should be reported to the nearest museum or Dyfed Archaeological Trust, The Shire Hall, Carmarthen Street, Llandeilo, Carmarthen SA19 6AF

4. Under no circumstances should visitors dig on or around any site. Any damage could result in prosecution.

5. It is an offence under the 1979 Ancient Monuments and Archaeological Areas Act to use metal detectors on or near scheduled ancient monuments. In addition, simple 'treasure hunting' near ancient monuments can well damage evidence to such an extent that archaeologists are unable to interpret it fully in the future.

Contents

Acknowledgements

The authors would like to thank all antiquarians, archaeologists and historians who have contributed articles to *Archaeologia Cambrensis* over the past 150 years. Be they living or dead, their efforts and enthusiasm are reflected throughout this book. Without their dedication, projects such as this would not be possible.

Many of the tomb plans have been adapted and re-drawn from a number of sources including Christopher Barker's excellent Monograph: *The Chambered Tombs of South West Wales* (1992) and Glyn Daniel's volume: *The Prehistoric Chambered Tombs of England and Wales* (1950).

The following people who directly helped with this book and who receive our sincere thanks are Debbie Wildgust at Tenby Museum, Martin Lewis & Stella Nash (The Trinity Press) and Sally Matthews (Tenbury Wells Library). Also, gratitude to Dr Trevor Kirk (Trinity College, Carmarthen), Jayne Pilkington (City of Bristol Archaeology Service), Alf Alderson and Philip Bennett of the Pembrokeshire Coast National Park Department who took valuable time to comment on the text. Finally thanks to Andy Johnson and Ron Shoesmith for their editorial comments; and to publishers Angus and Robertson, Sydney, for permission to reproduce photographs from Colin Simpson's *Plumes and Arrows: inside New Guinea.*

George & George
August 1997

Preparing the dead in the central uplands of Papua New Guinea—a clan leader is attended by relatives (from Simpson, 1953)

Preface

It was only during this century that the Neolithic period largely became associated with the introduction of agriculture and the construction of megalithic monuments. In 1954, Stuart Piggott first recognised a primary and secondary Neolithic, but for how long did these phases last? With the introduction of radiocarbon dating in the 1950s, the Neolithic began to expand and is now reckoned to span at least 2,000 years. In Britain the period begins around 4000 BC (calibrated years) and terminates around 2000 BC. These dates are based not just upon environmental criteria—the carbon-dating of domestic debris such as carbonised seeds, post holes, domesticated animal remains and wooden tools—but also upon the construction and use of megalithic monuments. Other factors too, are now considered. Recently, social, political and symbolic arguments have been incorporated into the overall picture.

The termination of the Neolithic may be identified, firstly, by a change of ideology and political infrastructure. This is apparent in the emergence of new burial practices and the relinquishment of the 'old order'—megalithic tombs are abandoned and, in some instances, their passages blocked with rubble, usually from the tomb itself. Secondly, these monuments of the old order are replaced by barrows, or simplified burial mounds. These were built to house one or two burials, whereas the old monuments were corporate tombs which would have contained many bodies. The decision to place these monuments in new locations also indicates a break with the past.

Identifying the beginning of the Neolithic is much more difficult, and conflicting ideas have been proposed to explain what the period actually represents. Very little in the way of settlement evidence survives, and the many different types of megalithic tomb, even within a small area such as south-west Wales, present a problem of chronology (which came first) and morphology (architecture).

What this book aims to do is identify the 'monumentality' of the area and place this into a landscape setting. Above all, it is hoped to highlight the importance of landscape and the need for a sense of belonging, or being-in-the-world. These monuments created an identity for the people who built and used them. Just as we associate ourselves with ancestry and our place within the world, so did the people of the Neolithic.

Throughout the text, we have used the dating method of BC (Before Christ) which also relates to corrected or calibrated radio-carbon dates. These differ from 'raw' dates, which are expressed in archaeological literature as bc, and may vary from the corrected BC dates by 2 - 300 years. The difference is due to fluctuations in the amount of radio-carbon decay after death by an animal or other organic remains, and this takes some consideration to calculate. In archaeological literature the term BP (Before Present) is also used, but usually only in an environmental context.

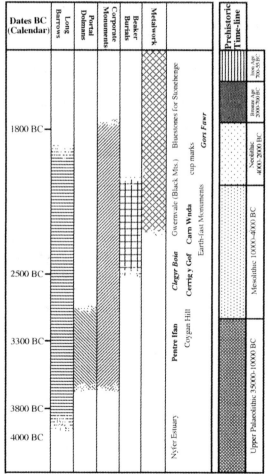

Time-line for Neolithic Monuments and Later Burials

Introduction:
Setting the Scene

I found myself always looking at the glacier. While we gathered wood and sedge root, it shone like a lake in winter and when we built our fires in the evening, it turned pink and then red in the sunset. Best of all, after dark but before the moon rose, the glacier made the night sky lighter, the same as fallen snow.

Elizabeth Marshall Thomas *Reindeer Moon*

At its maximum, 25-18,000 years ago, the immense Welsh ice sheet reached as far as St David's Head and Laugharne, leaving exposed only the southern portions of present-day Pembrokeshire and Carmarthenshire. Farther east, across Carmarthen Bay, only the tip of the Gower peninsula remained ice-free. It would be wrong, however, to imagine that prehistoric hunters were confined to these small areas. So much water was locked up in the glaciers that sea-levels dropped dramatically. As a result, Britain was at that time linked to the Continent, and much of Carmarthen Bay and the Bristol Channel was dry plain.

The coast line of south-west Wales is comparatively rich in prehistoric remains. A number of cave sites, such as those on Caldey Island, have yielded flint tools as well as the bones and teeth of hyena, woolly rhinocerous, mammoth, reindeer and horse. There is also compelling evidence that, despite the harsh conditions, these Palaeolithic (Old Stone Age) hunters, who probably only numbered

1

a handful of people, found time to bury their dead in a manner which suggests the existence of sophisticated religious beliefs. It was at the site of Paviland Cave on the Gower coast that, in 1823, the famous 'Red Lady' was discovered. Originally identified as female, the remains were later found to be those of a 25-year-old man. Who he was or how he died we do not know but he was clearly held in high enough esteem to warrant careful preparation for the afterlife. The body had been covered with red ochre, believed to symbolise re-birth, and within the 26,000-year-old burial were found objects of ivory and some perforated shells.

About 12,000 BC, the climate warmed and the ice started to retreat. As the glaciers melted, sea-levels rose by approximately 30m (Simmons and Tooley, 1981) until, around 6,500 BC, Britain became an island. The land, relieved of its great burden, also began to rise. The warmer conditions encouraged the spread of new plants and animals. A bare landscape of sub-Arctic tundra was gradually replaced by forests, dominated first by birch, then by hazel and pine, and finally by 'broad leaf' woodland. As the character of south-west Wales changed so did the lifestyle of its people. Some have suggested that animals began to be loose-herded and even selectively bred. In parts of Wales, fire may have been used to clear forest, encouraging the growth of young shoots especially attractive to deer. Also of dietary importance were fishing and the gathering of root plants, fruits and nuts. Experiments with horticulture may have eased the transition from hunting and gathering, which relies upon a natural abundance of plants and animals, to farming, involving the management and cultivation of non-indigenous crops, such as wheat and barley.

The Mesolithic (Middle Stone Age) (10,000 to 4,000 BC) is usually seen as a period of rapid population growth. Many people may have settled in base camps around the coasts, carrying out occasional hunting forays inland. Tell-tale mounds of discarded shells, known as middens, are frequently found in these coastal locations. Around Nab Head, more than 35,000 pieces of flint have been recovered, together with fragments of hazelnut shell and char-coal, indicating that deciduous forests, rich in plant foods and small game, were also being exploited. High concentrations of Late Mesolithic sea-pebble flint around the Afon Nyfer (Nevern) offer evidence that river valleys too were regarded as prime areas of economic activity. Each of the six scatters of flint tools and associated waste material that have been identified may represent special-purpose camps where flint-knappers plied their craft and presumably also fished. These areas may indicate 'working units' organised along kinship lines, with higher-ranking families reserving access to prime fishing sites. The more permanent settlements associated with the Mesolithic may have been similar to the Indian villages of the Pacific north-west coast of America.

As these developments continued, the treatment of the dead became increasingly sophisticated. During the Late Mesolithic (6,000 to 4,000 BC), occasional cemeteries began to appear (as evidenced in southern Scandinavia) suggesting greater social complexity, while the succeeding Neolithic period brought a further dramatic change in burial practice. In northern and western Europe, people began to build stone chambers or tombs to accommodate their dead. These consisted of a number of upright stones surmounted by a large, flat capstone and often covered by a mound made of earth or smaller stones. In south-west Wales, a total of 37 such 'houses for the dead' have survived to the present day. Some, although their covering mound has long since been weathered away, are remarkably well preserved; others have been reduced to little more than bramble-choked piles of rubble, their stones re-used by farmers as hanging posts for gates, to repair walls or fill holes in roads. Some tombs have been totally lost, their existence simply a matter of record in antiquarian studies. Others, perhaps, remain to be discovered.

When in use some 5,000 years ago, these tombs would have been periodically re-opened to receive fresh remains. No doubt such occasions were accompanied by ceremonies and perhaps feasting, as is the case in some parts of the world today. We do not know who exactly was granted burial rights, but it is doubtful that these rights were extended to the whole community. It is more likely that those interred were members of an hereditary élite who took up final residence in the tomb after a period of exposure to the elements (excarnation), or preliminary burial, during which their flesh, often regarded as 'polluting' among contemporary peoples, was stripped from the bone, the 'sacred' element of the corpse. This obsession with removing the 'wetness' of decomposing flesh is common throughout the modern world. In the Tauri River region of Papua New Guinea, for example, fresh corpses are smoked on a special platform constructed inside the hut of the deceased. Clan leaders (big men) and young warriors—but not children or the elderly—are treated in this way, and it is the task of relatives to tend the fire during the smoking process. This can last up to six months. Initially the ritual is charged with emotion, but soon the body loses its identity and becomes known by a special name. When the curing is complete, the dry, leathery corpse—wrapped in bark and now weighing only 15-20kg—is carried out of the village to a high rocky ledge, where it is propped up with arrows and painted with red ochre, symbolising blood, fertility and rebirth.

In addition to being repositories for the dead, the Neolithic tombs also stood as monuments, reminding the living that earlier generations had been born, lived and died within sight of the tomb. In other words, they helped to create a sense of history, a sense of belonging. Inside the tombs, the ancestors would, if respectfully treated, be allies in the continual struggle for survival.

Many have associated the appearance of these monuments with the introduction of a new way of life—farming. Was this the result of newcomers moving into the area, colonists who crossed over from the Continent or possibly from Ireland bringing a new economy and a new set of beliefs with them? If so, what happened to the native hunter/gatherers—were they, like the North American Indians, relegated to the status of 'second-class citizens?' One claim is that they became 'guides, porters and perhaps stockmen for the subsequent Neolithic people' (Stanford, 1991). Alternatively, the migration may have been one of ideas rather than of people, similar to the process of 'Americanisation' which has influenced the lifestyle of millions across the globe. As the shift towards farming gathered pace, people needed to mark out their territory more clearly. The monuments may have been saying: 'This land is ours because it belonged to our ancestors!'

Towards the end of the Neolithic, a new wave of ideas began to effect further social change, giving rise to a transitional phase between Neolithic and Bronze Age society (Savory, 1980, 228). It was once believed the small, highly-decorated beakers sometimes

Preparing the dead: the smoking and curing of ancestors in the central uplands of Papua New Guinea (from Simpson, 1953)

found in Late Neolithic burials arrived in Britain with the so-called 'Beaker Folk' as part of an 'invasion package' which also included copper daggers, archers' 'wrist-guards' and barbed-and-tanged arrowheads. Once again the invasion now tends to be seen principally as a movement of ideas. Some have suggested that the Beaker period was one of 'standstill' in the development of an agricultural society. When the corporate monumentality of the Late Neolithic ended, many of the old monuments either had their entrances blocked up and were abandoned, or in some cases were re-used for Beaker burials. An example is the long chambered cairn at Gwernvale in the Black Mountains which was blocked with rubble towards the middle of the third millennium. In some instances, burials were incorporated within the blocking material. This practice may either represent the final act of Neolithic mortuary ritual or a new means of controlling the wealth and prestige of the interred, the destruction of the monument in fact being part of its reconstitution. Along with this phase of abandonment/destruction came the desertion of camps and enclosures. Pollen evidence suggests woodland species began to re-establish themselves over previous cultivated/cleared areas, a phenomenon apparent not only in this part of Wales, but throughout Britain.

Associated with the decline of corporate monumentality came a new ideology, its underlying symbolism associated with the rising and setting of the sun and moon. Arguably, these themes were already present during the Neolithic, as suggested by a tendency towards an east/west orientation of passages and mounds. However, the interest in celestial movements was taken a stage further during the Late Neolithic/Early Bronze Age with the construction of stone circles, henge monuments and stone alignments. We have argued (1996) that such alignments, especially in this area of Britain, constituted processional paths representing the journey from death to the afterlife. Alignments also incorporated round barrows or cairns, earth or stone structures which, during the second half of the third millennium, took over as the principal burial monuments. Like the Neolithic chambered tombs, these new monuments form clusters. However, the location of barrows, either on the valley floor or on the tops of hills, is quite different from the distribution of earlier monuments. It is quite obvious that construction methods used, design and landscape positioning represent a different cultural and symbolic package.

The Neolithic

Monuments and Mindscapes

What is a landscape? There are of course the obvious physical features—headlands, crags, river valleys, estuaries. To these one must add the human mind, for it is our experience of the 'raw material' provided by nature which establishes a landscape. Landscape is not a neutral arrangement of physical forms, it is something we respond to emotionally, a place where the presence of previous generations can be felt. Among the Kunwinjku Aborigines of western Arnhem Land, Australia, each clan is bound to its territory by beliefs linking the spirits of the dead with certain sacred places created from the body parts of ancestral beings. Articulating these beliefs is the task of the Kunwinjku artist. His medium is a style of narrative painting which depicts the ancestral beings in the form of certain animals, regarded by the Kunwinjku as valuable sources of food. The paintings operate on a number of levels. At its most basic, the art is a medium of instruction whereby the young learn, as we would learn from a diagram or illustration, how to recognise significant species. On a symbolic level, however, the paintings possess a range of meanings which only become fully apparent to the initiated. At this level of understanding, the body of the animal becomes a metaphor for the cultural world of the Kunwinjku. It becomes, in a sense, a means of orientation, a cultural map. The geometric motifs used by the artist to represent the internal organs and skeleton of the animal now take on an added symbolic meaning, representing particular spiritually-powerful places within the landscape. It is here that, following the performance of ritual songs and dances, the dead take up residence, replenishing the spirit of the ancestral being.

A similar sense of the inter-relationship of landscape, the spirit world and human history and well-being is apparent in Madagascar, where the ancestors have a pervasive influence upon everyday affairs and are associated in particular with rice and cattle, the two most important components of the island's traditional economy. A tradition of communal burial exists on the island; the Malagasy believe being buried alone inhibits the flow of vitality from ancestors to living descendants, affecting the success of the group. Before remains can be placed within the tomb, however, the polluting 'wet' flesh must be separated from the sacred bones. This is sometimes achieved by initial burial followed by exhumation some time later. As the bones of the newly-interred intermingle with those of its kinsmen so the identity of the individual merges with the memory of the ancestors. This process can be hastened by the customary act of 'turning the dead', a ritual which involves periodically opening the tomb and rewrapping the deceased in a new burial shroud, the elaborately-woven *lamba mena* (Mack, 1986, 75). The *famadihana* is far from being a solemn occasion. Music is played and the corpse is carried around by its descendants and danced with before being returned to its resting place. The original *lamba mena*, now much decomposed, is used by relatives of the deceased for copulation, thereby becoming a link between the living and the dead: death regenerates life. The tomb usually serves an extended family, although there are areas within the uplands where entire villages use the monument. Architecturally, these structures are very similar to the collective burial monuments of Neolithic Europe. Furthermore, there are striking similarities in terms of location. The tombs of the Merina people, who inhabit the central plateau of Madagascar, tend to be visible and easily accessible. They are built close to villages and the bones within the chambers are regarded as essential to the success of the clan and the continued fertility of its lands. Tombs in the south-east of the island, however, are deliberately hidden away from the living in sacred groves. Cutting down trees around the monument may be considered taboo and access is only possible with the permission of ritual specialists. In one case, graves are located in marshes around the estuary of the Manambondro river and are only accessible by canoe (Mack, 1986, 82). A very similar pattern of diverse landscape settings occurs in south-west Wales. Around Newport, for example, monuments occupy locations ranging from coasts to inland valley-floor sites. Some, namely the coastal monuments of Llech-y-Tribedd and Trellyffant, appear to be deliberately hidden from sight of the sea; while further inland, Bedd-yr-Afanc lies unobtrusively in marshy ground deep within a U-shaped valley and, like the Manambondro graves, may have been seasonally surrounded by water. In both cases, the deceased are segregated from the living on 'islands' of the dead. By contrast, Pentre Ifan is situated on rising ground in full view of the visually-striking Mynydd Preseli.

Finally, for the Sumba islanders of Indonesia, the coastal locations of their 'houses of the dead' are highly symbolic places, each monument remaining in use for many centuries. Before reaching their final resting place, the dead are paraded through the village and treated with increasing reverence as they approach the stone-chambered tomb.

These observations and the wider theme of death and the landscape will be developed throughout the following pages. We suggest that socio-ritual knowledge and the consciousness and manner in which people perceive objects within their own surroundings is fundamental to formulating a sense of belonging. The building of a chambered tomb is in itself not sufficient to statement the landscape. Focusing upon one small point—the monument—does not enable one to construct a cognitive and visual perception of an entire landscape. Many other components: valley spurs, rivers, scarp edges, slopes etc., are required to bring about a visual totality. By focusing upon its outer space, the tomb becomes an integral part of a greater outer space—the landscape—and the monument becomes part of that visual impact. The tomb may not be visually apparent, but local people are aware of its existence. This is controlled and manipulated by knowledge—ritual knowledge. The French architect, Le Corbusier (1923, in Frampton, 1992), one of the main exponents of functionalism in architecture, established the idea that architecture is not a physical medium but an awareness of concept, design and ideology. He states:

'By the use of inert materials and starting from conditions more or less utilitarian, you have established certain relationships which have aroused my emotions. This is Architecture.'

Such emotions form part both of a sense of belonging and a familiarity and sense of association with landscape.

Our main focus throughout the book is on the Neolithic, the New Stone Age, a period when it is believed the first agricultural communities became established. It is important to emphasise that the shift from hunting and gathering to farming was no 'overnight affair'. People would not all at once have ditched their hunting paraphernalia and taken up the plough. Rather, elements of the two subsistence strategies probably long co-existed. After all, why go to the trouble of growing your own food when there are richly-stocked waters on your doorstep? Neolithic chambered tombs are found throughout northern and western Europe. Yet simply because a common practice of monument-building was in existence does not mean the underlying ideas were equally consistent over this wide geographical area. Local traditions were probably much more important than global ideology. In other words, the monuments offered a new medium for the expression of traditional values and perceptions. While conforming broadly to a well-established pattern, a blueprint, these monuments exhibit many localised traits in design and orientation. Adopting megalithic architecture was a means of keeping abreast of developments within the wider world, while at the same time reinforcing one's own sense of local identity.

A Mesolithic in Transition
During the Late Glacial period most of north-western Europe consisted of a harsh tundra-steppe environment. This landscape attracted many large tundra-foraging mammals, such as reindeer (*Rangifer tarandus*) and elk (*Alces alces*) which, in turn, attracted the first 'specialist' hunters. Gronnow (1985, 131) suggests that small hunting parties set up short-term seasonal camps along well established 'ancestral' reindeer migration trails. The two sites of Meiendorf and Stellmoor, both in northern Germany, are examples of 'mass kill' encampments used during the late Upper Palaeolithic

(Gronnow, 1985, 130). At Stellmoor 'A', there is evidence of reindeer skinning, butchering, filleting, marrow-fracturing and possible crushing and boiling of bone (Gronnow, 1985, 134). Similar types of carcass utilisation are seen throughout the Danish Mesolithic (Nash, 1992). Here, red deer (*Capreolus elephas*) and even killer whale (*Orca gladiator*) were used to full advantage. It appears nothing was wasted. Farther north, evidence from the Norwegian uplands is scarce. A large number of reindeer pitfalls (traps) have been located within the Setesdal Mountains (east of Stravanger). Constructed of drystone walling, these are situated along reindeer migration routes and date from the Scandinavian Iron Age—subfossil evidence dates from about 300 BC (1988, 104). A number of lithic scatters, representing possible settlements located along the Central Mountains of western Norway, have been recognised close to upland lakes. In addition, fire-cracked stone mounds, used for cooking and possibly indicating upland winter settlement (dating between 3,300 and 3,500 BC), have been found in Västerbotten County, close to lakes and upland tributaries.

Closer to home, Caseldine (1990, 35) has recognised two different settlement environs in Wales: one upland, the other coastal. The vast majority of the sites in the south-west fall into the latter category. However, it is unlikely that these coastal communities ignored the rich uplands and the opportunities they offered for seasonal big-game hunting. Potters Cave, on Caldey Island, has yielded remains of red deer and also of dog, the latter possibly assisting hunters in the kill; and both red and roe deer have been discovered at the cave of Ogof Carreg Hir, on St Govan's Head. In addition, there is evidence that hunters were deliberately modifying their environment in order to maximise returns. Fire may have been used, for instance, to clear extensive upland areas, a strategy which would have encouraged the growth of young shoots attractive to grazing herds of deer. The discovery of charcoal in wetland deposits (mor profiles) around Mynydd Preseli, the Black Mountains and upland North Wales points to a long-term hunting strategy based upon control of food resources within a defined hunting territory. Caseldine (1990, 36) suggests that such an open-heathland strategy was in operation between 6,000 and 4,000 BC. Upland clearances were probably seasonal, taking place during the autumn to encourage spring regeneration. Radiocarbon dates of 2,900 BC have been obtained from a charcoal layer within blanket peat from the upland site of Waun-Fignen-Felen. Although this date is rather late, it is nonetheless important to note that the uplands were being modified by human activity well before the Bronze Age, when extensive forest clearance took place.

Given the rich marine resources available to coastal communities and the opportunities for foraging and for the hunting of smaller animals, large-scale game hunts may well have been economically unviable. Ethnographic evidence suggests 'big game' means 'big commitment'. In many modern hunter-gatherer societies, the killing and eating of larger mammals plays only a minor role in day-to-day activities. Lee (1968) shows that the dietary intake of the !Kung bush people of the Kalahari, Botswana, consists of 60-80% vegetable foods. The remaining 20-40% is made up mainly of small invertebrate animals, especially grubs and larvae, both of which are high in protein. Of course, the killing of animals in such societies is considered more than just a means of providing food. Studies of forest hunter-gatherers, for example, emphasise the symbolic role of meat. The Baka people of central Cameroon carry out monkey hunts on a largely ritual basis. The consumption of meat appears to play a secondary role in daily food intake (Turnbull, 1962). The Aborigines of central and northern Australia rarely kill and eat large marsupials. Indeed, great sorrow is expressed when the life of such a creature is taken. Animals are a particularly important component of Aboriginal society, not as a food source, but as a symbolic-ritual component of daily life. They feature in all Aboriginal stories and fables and are predominant in the creation of the 'dream time' (Reed, 1965). Animals in these cultures are deemed to be good for thinking rather than for eating.

Apart from its symbolic and ritual uses, meat may also be of political significance. The equal sharing of meat in most hunter-gatherer societies dispels the notion of hierarchy and economic value: the group becomes one. In !Kung and Mbuti society, the ownership of a killed animal cannot be regarded as ownership in the true sense of the word. Weapons are usually made by other individuals of the group and loaned to the hunter, thus reducing the legitimate right of direct ownership. The meat can therefore belong to more than one person and the sharing allows everyone in the group to participate (Lee, 1979).

Among the numerous coastal sites utilized by Mesolithic communities in south-west Wales are Nab Head and Dinas Head. Included among some 35,000 flint pieces discovered within the former area was a shale bracelet, now on display in Tenby Museum. The presence of such an object indicates that, in addition to purely economic concerns, Mesolithic people devoted time to the production of valuables, items of symbolic rather than functional importance.

Plate 1 The shale bracelet found at Nab Head

Mesolithic flint scatters found some way upstream on a number of tributaries within the area suggest these waterways served not only as routes for migrating fish but also as highways for mobile Mesolithic and later Neolithic groups. The authors have located two such lithic scatters 0.8 and 1.2km up the Afon Nyfer (Nevern) valley within stratified river deposits. The flint is coarser and occurs in smaller quantities than that from Nab Head, yet these assemblages reflect an ideal Mesolithic environment, where advanced hunter/gatherers could prey on freshwater and migratory fish, seasonally controlling their activities to take advantage of spawning salmon and trout.

The largest selection of lithics was recovered towards the estuary and the open sea overlooking Strumble Head. Finds included much waste material, and tools such as scrapers, blades and cores. It is generally assumed that the sea level of the late Mesolithic was similar to that of today, meaning the producers of the tools were no doubt also fishermen who gutted and prepared the fish as it was caught. Given the proximity of the Coetan Arthur monument, roughly 25m east of the present shoreline, it seems likely that marine resources continued to be exploited during the Neolithic, in conjunction with limited inland hunting/gathering and agriculture. Leach, for example, recognised 'kitchen middens' near Tenby, which yielded 'quantities of shells of many species of (chiefly edible) marine mollusca' in association with a Neolithic leaf-shaped arrowhead and 'bones and teeth of recent wild and domesticated animals' (Leach, 1932).

In broad terms, the Mesolithic was a period of gradual change in settlement behaviour, from the use of temporary encampments, associated with moving around the countryside on hunting, gathering and foraging expeditions, to more permanent bases. Although the abandonment of one type of economy and the adoption of another cannot always be clearly identified, this change, possibly more than any other, provided the incentive to adopt agriculture, the basis of the succeeding Neolithic economy.

From Foraging to Farming: The Neolithic

The Neolithic (New Stone Age) is the latest of the three stone ages and represents the introduction of agriculture. It is now thought that this revolution began about 10,000 years ago in the Fertile Crescent—present day Lebanon, Israel and Syria. By about 4,000 BC, there is evidence of small garden-style allotments throughout the fertile valleys of Western Europe, although many parts of Britain would still have been covered by dense forest. However, it seems that by this time, domesticated sheep, continental cattle, pigs and seed corn were being imported into Britain, now an island. But the shift to agriculture was no overnight event. During the preceding Mesolithic period (10,000-4,000 BC), there is evidence for the controlled herding and corralling of wild animals, in addition to the seasonal harvesting of wild fruits, roots and nuts. The rigid divide often believed to exist between a hunter/gatherer way of life and a farming economy is therefore rather misleading. The

Plate 2 Collection of polished stone axes from south-west Wales

evidence suggests a gradual process of economic and social change, developments which may have included the emergence of hereditary élites.

A number of single 'prestige' chance-finds indicate that these emergent élites were possibly involved in trading alliances or seasonal expeditions outside south-west Wales. In all, around 175 polished stone and flint axes have been recovered, the pieces having either been quarried, shaped and polished at source or else taken away as 'rough-outs' and finished locally. These items were undoubtedly prized for their prestige value. It has been demonstrated that if used, most polished stone axes would shatter. So, although ostensibly functional, these objects in fact symbolised power and prestige within a stratified society. The origins of such items, in a few cases as far afield as Cornwall and Cumbria, suggest valuable time had to be set aside for lengthy exchange visits, the organisation of which would undoubtedly have been socially and politically complex. Indeed, judging by the large number of Neolithic monuments and surface flint and stone found in this part of Wales, axe-collecting and production may have involved alliances between a number of groups bound together by marriage and/or common ancestry. A selection of fine examples of green-stone axes has been found throughout the region, the stone originating in the Penzance area (Cornwall). Again, it is not known whether the axes were shaped at source or within south-west Wales itself, although evidence, in the form of flint waste, suggests rough-outs were being brought into the area for re-working. There was also a major local source for the production of axes in the Preseli Mountains (See Appendix D).[1]

As with other parts of Britain, the evidence for Neolithic settlement in south-west Wales is slight and only two well-documented sites are known. These are Clegyr Boia, to the west of St David's, close to the monuments of Carn Llidi and Coetan Arthur; and Coygan Camp, a multi-period site near Laugharne.

Clegyr Boia is set within rectangular ramparts, measuring 100m by 25m, that may be of Iron Age date. The settlement, excavated in

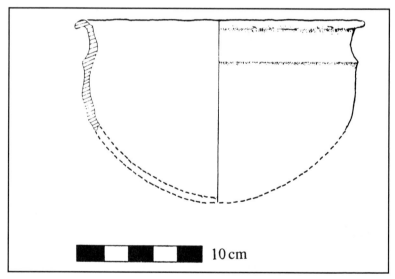

Fig. 1 Late Neolithic Style Pottery from the Clegyr Boia Settlement (drawn by A. Williams, 1980)

1. We are grateful to Jenny Hall of Cambria Archaeology for information concerning axe distribution in south-west Wales from Sites and Monuments records.

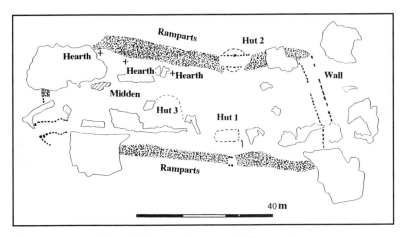

Plan 1 The Settlement of Clegyr Boia
(adapted from Barker, 1992 and Williams, 1953)

1943, consists of two Neolithic house structures, a fire pit and a midden (Williams, 1953, 24-9). An earlier excavation revealed a possible third hut, located centrally within the rampart area (Baring-Gould, 1903). Outside the settlement area, a large number of Mesolithic flint scatters suggest continuous occupation of the peninsula for well over 4,000 years.

One of the houses is oval, the other rectangular. The rectangular structure (7m by 3m) comprised two rows of posts, which may have supported a timber roof. An 'unused pit' investigated inside this structure by Audrey Williams was compared by the excavator to similar pits discovered under the Pentre Ifan monument. She also suggested a link between the two sites on the basis of pottery evidence.

The oval hut yielded evidence of extensive burning. Barker (1992) has suggested that the burning, plus the deposition of pottery in each of the contexts, indicates possible ritual abandonment. We would argue that the settlement and the two nearby monuments are contemporary, and that the former may have suffered natural abandonment towards the end of the Neolithic, only being re-occupied in the Iron Age. Pottery from the oval hut appears to be identical to examples found in the rectangular structure and in the midden to the west. Three different Neolithic pottery styles have been identified in all, and are similar to wares found in Cornwall, Southern Ireland and the Wessex region. The evidence suggests that a possible exchange network linked these areas. Barker (1992) proposes a Middle Neolithic (4,300 to 3,300 BC) date for the pottery from Clegyr Boia. Recovered from the floors of two huts were shouldered bowls, a number of animal bones, mainly of wild cattle, and limpet shells.

A series of hearths to the west of the oval hut yielded a flint arrow-head and a partly-polished stone axe of gritty volcanic tuff (Houlder, 1988). Limpet shells, pottery, and oak and birch charcoal were recovered from the midden. Cattle bone was found in both huts. The bone, together with the shells, suggest that the people of Clegyr Boia existed on a mixed economy of hunting/gathering/fishing with an element of domesticated herding. The settlement may have supported only two or three small family units at any one time.

The second settlement identified in south-west Wales is located on Coygan Hill and dates from the Early Neolithic, around 3,750 BC. An earlier phase of Mesolithic occupation has also been suggested (Castleden, 1992). Located close to the sea and the mouths of the Afon Tywi (Towy) and Taf, Coygan Camp revealed a number of datable organics, including charred hazelnut shells and animal bone recovered from a small fire-pit (Taylor, 1980). The bone and the shells, which date to about 3,700 BC, suggest hunting and gathering remained an important component of daily Neolithic life.

It is not, however, the economic or settlement evidence that predominates during the Neolithic, but, for the first time, monuments commemorating the dead. Elaborate chambered tombs made of large stones, or megaliths, dominate the landscape of south-west Wales and elsewhere. Originally, many of these monuments were covered by a mound, leaving only the entrance or forecourt area and passage visible. In common with present-day religious buildings, areas of the tomb would have been restricted to particular religious or social strata. But the archaeological evidence suggests these chambers were more than mere repositories for the dead, having a social and political, as well as a symbolic, function.

Approximately 3km to the north of the Clegyr Boia settlement are the two tombs of Carn Llidi and Cotean Arthur that belong to the St David's Group of monuments. These are 'earth-fast' in form, having one end of their capstone resting on the edge of a pit while the other end is supported by upright stones. These tombs are small enough to have been constructed and managed by a small group. To the east of both monuments is a series of prehistoric field systems which are arguably of a later date. Nevertheless, apart from the rearing of cattle and fishing of seasonal marine fauna, including mammals such as dolphin and seal, communities on this peninsula may have relied upon the produce from small gardens, although there is no pollen record to indicate this. The choice of different economic resources would have created a buffer against the changeable seasonal climate prevailing in this part of Wales.

Larger-scale monument building would have required a more careful logistical strategy and neighbouring communities may have assisted in projects such as Longhouse and Pentre Ifan. These would have required many thousands of working hours to complete. By gathering together small communities from around the locality for co-operative projects, a collective identity could have been established—hence the similarity between many of the monuments in the region.

Death in the Neolithic
It has been argued that during the Neolithic 'a body might receive successive treatment of ... different kinds—excarnation, removal, redeposition, rearrangement, and so on' (Kinnes, 1992). At Quanterness, a large Neolithic 'stalled cairn' on Orkney, the excavator, Colin Renfrew, suggested 'bodies had first been either buried or exposed elsewhere, so that the flesh and ligaments decomposed and the bones became disarticulated' (Renfrew, 1979). He refers to Swanton (1946), who discussed a similar ritual practised by the Indians of the south-eastern United States. There, a recently-deceased village chief would be exhumed after a year, his bones taken by 'Turkey Buzzard Men'. The remains, now defleshed, would be wrapped in a symbolic chequered mat, similar to the Madagascar *lamba mena,* and deposited within a specially-constructed 'bone house'. Later, the bones would be used in the *kut-naha* ceremony, which, commencing at nightfall, would involve the assembled entourage walking six times around a ceremonial fire

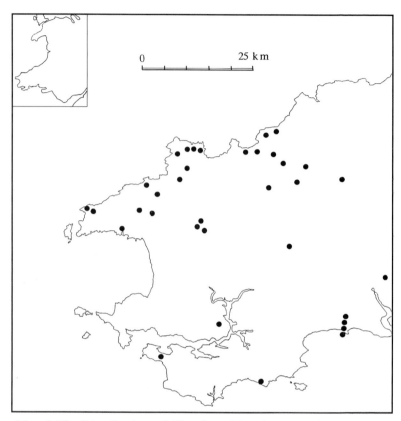

Map 1 The Distribution of Chambered Tombs in south-west Wales

before placing the chief's remains within a mound. The evidence from Quanterness suggests bodies were excarnated for up to three years after death and the cairn periodically opened up, probably on special feasting days, to deposit new ancestors. It has been estimated, on the basis of limited excavation, that this monument was in intensive use for about 200 years. The bones belonging to 394 individuals, with an average age of 20-25 years, were discovered within the chambered area. We suggest that Quanterness was the final resting place for these individuals, who, following excarnation, would have been moved around the landscape through a number of smaller satellite monuments. When they had completed their journey and period of transition, the bones would be placed within the larger monument and no longer recognised as individual human beings.

A similar nucleated pattern is apparent in south-west Wales. For example, Pentre Ifan, Carreg Sampson and Garn Turne are all large megalithic monuments with chambers able to accommodate the bones from nearby tombs. All three have panoramic views of the surrounding landscape. Smaller tombs close by do not. The larger monuments in each cluster may have been the final resting places of bones that had first circulated around these satellite tombs; the circulation of remains perhaps imitating the seasonal movements of hunter/gatherer ancestors. Unfortunately, the acidic nature of the soils in this region has long since destroyed any traces of bone.

The south-west Wales monuments conform to a number of basic architectural rules. Firstly, they all possess a chamber comprising a series of upright stones (orthostats) and a large capstone. Capstones vary greatly in size, from a few hundred kilograms, *e.g.* Carn Besi, to well over 60 tons at Garn Turne—both monuments forming part of the Inland Pembrokeshire Group. Elsewhere, there is evidence for two chambers, referred to sometimes as a double dolmen, whilst at Cerrig y Gof, near Newport, five small chambers are set within a round mound. The double dolmens may be considered later developments of Neolithic burial practice, and may even act as corporate monuments, like the Severn-Cotswold tombs on the Black Mountains and along the Gower coast.

The chambers of Neolithic monuments appear to be governed by the type of ritual activity that took place within and around them. For example, at Pentre Ifan and Carreg Samson, the chamber areas are large enough to accommodate ceremonies and to ritually deposit human remains. The double chambers at St Elvis Farm, The Hanging Stone, Parc-y-Llyn and Carn Llidi were found to contain the remains of at least two bodies inside each tomb. Further east, at the Severn-Cotswold tomb of Parc-le-Breos-Cwm on the Gower, 24 individuals were interred in four chambers. The remains consisted of disarticulated bone that was 'much broken and in no regular arrangement' (Lubbock, 1871). By contrast, many of the 'earth fast' monuments on Strumble Head are so small and exposed that the chamber could not house a complete corpse.

*Plate 3 Small rectangular chamber at Parc-le-Breos-Cwm,
Gower: compartmentalising the dead*

Does the ritual deposition of bone in tombs such as Parc-le-
Breos-Cwm indicate the exclusive use of the monument by a hier-
archical dynastic elite, or are the interred merely part of an egali-
tarian society? It is quite obvious that the single chambers represent
a different ideology, relating to both burial and social structure,
from that of multiple deposition. However, there is also the question of multiple burial within a single chamber. Burial in this case
follows either excarnation or cremation. This type of deposition is

very much a Late Neolithic trait and may form the ideology behind the single burial tradition of the Early Bronze Age.

Another recurrent feature of tomb morphology is the mound or cairn surrounding the chamber. Sadly, agricultural operations in the recent past have resulted in the ploughing-out of many mounds. At best, all that remains is a slight rise. Often there is no trace of a mound at all. The 'earth fast' monuments, smaller, and probably Late Neolithic (3,300 to 2,300 BC) tombs, may never have possessed a substantial mound, having just a small cairn wall in front of the chamber. The siting of each of these monuments, close to a rock outcrop, would disguise the tomb in its surroundings. This is important if a symbolic rather than a visual impact is to be created.

Comparisons have been drawn between Neolithic chambered tombs and the longhouses constructed by farming communities on the Continent. Similarly, certain clans of eastern Madagascar traditionally regarded their tombs as 'houses of the dead'. Constructed inside a fenced-off area within the village, these tombs were identical to dwellings and even contained the personal belongings of the deceased. The dead were buried in trenches and grouped according to age, status and gender (Mack, 1986, 77).

A direct parallel may be drawn between the linear form of the long house and that of the later Neolithic 'passage grave'. It has been argued that a 'passage grave' tradition flourished in this area of Wales, albeit small and localised and nowhere near the monumental proportions of Anglesey and Ireland. In other regions of Wales tombs with passages also exist but they are isolated examples and follow no direct pattern—they appear to be of purely local design and construction. Nevertheless, passage graves, where they do occur, follow one simple rule: the passage provides a space, a 'liminal' space between the living and the dead. By moving the body or the remains through the passage, the deceased undertakes the final mortal journey to its resting place—the chamber. Access to the passage—small, uninviting and mysterious—would have been restricted, and only select members of the group allowed to 'travel' its length to the inner sanctum of the chamber, where secret burial rites may have been performed. At Parc-le-Breos-Cwm on the Gower peninsula, large protruding horns either side of the

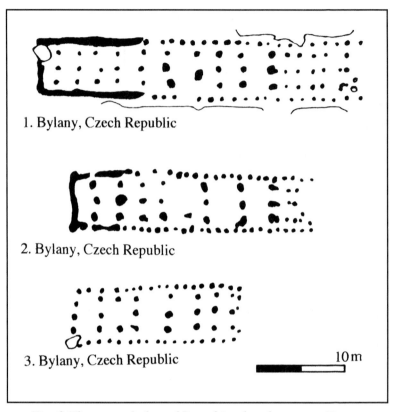

1. Bylany, Czech Republic

2. Bylany, Czech Republic

3. Bylany, Czech Republic   10m

*Fig. 2 The ground plan of Danubian longhouses or Domus
(Source: Hodder, 1990)*

facade and passage entrance area added to the secrecy and visual restriction of such ceremonies. Such a facade is also visible at Pentre Ifan and Garn Turne. Both of these tombs suggest restricted visual access, as the horns narrow towards the entrance. A similar pattern occurs with the passage grave tradition in central southern Sweden and Denmark (Tilley, 1991). Here, the entrance to the passage is narrower than the chamber doorway. Both features achieve similar effects.

Gradually, there is a shift from disarticulated remains to articulated male burials, suggesting adult males were being granted privileged access to the tombs (Hodder, 1990; Bradley, 1984). There are also attempts to hide or mask knowledge of the tomb's contents using devices such as blocking, false entrances and constricted access. Such control of knowledge may have been linked to control in other areas of life and to a male-dominated society. In south-west Wales, a possible shift from corporate monumentality to single-status burials is reflected in a trend away from the construction and use of large chambered tombs towards a preference for small, insignificant 'earth fast' monuments. The former are highly visible; whereas, the latter merge with the landscape. It is quite obvious that the single chambers represent a different ideology in both burial and social structure from that of multiple burial and are very much a Late Neolithic trait.

Socialising Death within the Landscape

The obvious affinity with the sea that we find among the monument-builders of south-west Wales suggests that many of the ideas which accompanied the spread of the Neolithic were not fully understood in this and in other areas of Wales. We know, for example, that monuments elsewhere in Britain have their mound, chamber and passage (where present) aligned in a consistent way and that they observe certain architectural rules. Many of the marine monuments in Wales, however, are locally-oriented in relation to the sea, possibly acknowledged as a ritual and symbolic ancestor, and to certain prominent topographic features, such as mountain peaks and headlands. Rivers also seem to have acted as magnets, influencing the distribution and orientation of monuments. This is apparent particularly in the location of chambered tombs within the inland Black Mountains group. Here, monuments are deliberately placed close to the tributaries of two major rivers: the Usk and Wye. With the exception of Ffostyll North and South, near Talgarth, each monument is surrounded by a network of small streams, possibly acting as symbolic and political boundaries. Such observations suggest continuity within local traditions of landscape perception and a certain degree of isolation from mainstream Neolithic ideology.

Hidden Architecture

In addition, a number of tomb clusters also possess territorial relationships. These clusters tend to comprise one valley-orientated monument and another aligned to a particular topographic feature. Major rivers and streams appear to be territorial boundaries. For example, Pentre Ifan and Bedd-yr-Afanc, orientated to the valley (or river) are allied with Coetan Arthur, which is aligned towards the Afon Nyfer estuary. Cerrig y Gof, also within the same group 'acts' as a nucleus for all the major topographic features within the vicinity. Each monument appears to take on a special role within the cluster. Other monuments in other groups throughout Wales 'play' identical roles (Tilley, 1994).

Recently it has been suggested (Thomas, 1993) that early tombs played an important role in 'presencing the ancestors' into the surrounding landscape; in other words, they helped return the dead whence they came. This, however, is only part of a more complex story. It is the tomb itself, rather than the socio-political-symbolic nature of the body, which is of paramount importance in both design and location. A relationship between design and the body has also been proposed. Christopher Tilley (1993) and Julian Thomas (1993) have suggested tomb architecture around the Gulf of Morbihan, Brittany, resembles the human rib cage. They suggest further that megalithic art represents parts of the human skeleton. A plausible idea—but there is a problem in that tomb design appears to be in direct conflict with the body, which is organic: it decays and eventually turns to dust. By contrast, tomb architecture opposes body symbolism. It does not decay but remains as a monument, a constant reminder of the dead. Furthermore, by disarticulating the human skeleton within the tomb, one is purposely dehumanising space, giving rise to a series of structural oppositions based upon outer and inner tomb space, for example life v death, public v private, natural v mechanical, social v ritual, and so on.

The siting of tombs has been interpreted as a form of 'statementing' the landscape—a means of turning a space into a place. Both ritual and political knowledge come into play to make this place special. We would add that to outsiders each of the monuments is hidden; organic and incognito in relation to its surroundings. Even monuments such as Pentre Ifan and the Longhouse would originally have had a covering mound. Today, only part of the monument is visible, usually a few uprights and a fragmented capstone, the 'frame' or 'skeleton', the rib-cage identified by

Thomas and Tilley (1993). The frame becomes structurally and visually opposed to the landscape; angular and mechanical, it clashes with the irregular, chaotic, organic landscape, suggesting order, control and design. However, during the Neolithic, the frame (or skeleton) would have possessed 'flesh'. Each capstone, each upright would have been hidden by an earthen mound or cairn, thereby creating an homogeneous whole. The monument thus became part of the landscape rather than opposing it, while within, nature is, in part, rejected. Here, a social and symbolic order dominates. The space becomes legitimated and clinical. Although the raw materials (*i.e.* stone and earth) are natural, the construction is not. One can see how the 'rawness' of individual materials is applied to modern architecture.

Creating an Organic Architecture
Many of architect Frank Lloyd Wright's ideas on the use of materials in an organic form are relevant to a discussion of mechanical and natural forms within the landscape (Frampton, 1992). For example the Winslow House, River Forest, Illinois, presents a metaphor of private and public space. Wright's design projects two meanings (or aspects): an irregular rural facade (the merging of the garden space with the random, organic fascia) and that of the urban frontage, which is ordered, symmetrical and mechanical. The extended space around the house is often organised in a similar fashion. The front garden is neat, tidy and regimented, while, to the rear, the garden is a place for storage, domestication—a place of privacy.

A more spectacular example is the Falling Water concept at Bear Run, Illinois, built in 1936. Again, the design typifies the organic principles whereby concrete and glass are applied to an organic design—where 'the place of the living is fused into nature' (Frampton, 1992). The building incorporates the principles of falling water. In both instances, Wright considered the materials used did not necessarily have to be organic in the literal sense of the word. Many of his buildings were in fact made from concrete blocking. It is the way in which the materials are used that creates an organic architecture. Therefore, one can not contemplate the stone frame of any tomb as being organic. These structures are truly mechanical in form. It is the mound material, the outer space that is organic. However, this form is contrived so as to organise the visual impact of landscape and, in particular, prominent topographic features.

Replicating Landscape

We have suggested that many of the features of the inner and outer space of the tomb are orientated towards various features within the landscape. We now argue that the tomb plan and layout replicate that landscape—it draws the outside within. The mechanical form metamorphoses the inner space into a stylised ritual map, in that certain topographic features are symbolically mapped and incorporated within the tomb plan. So, although the inner space opposes the outer space, the outer space when replicated within, becomes manipulated and controlled—the landscape is subdued.

To place these ideas into context, we have chosen the tombs of the Newport Group. With regards to actual replication, each monument has developed its own unique morphology. It appears either to be valley-orientated or to point towards a particular topographic feature, such as Carningli, Dinas Head or the lower Nyfer (Nevern) Valley. Six of the tombs actually do both. Features such as rivers, valleys, upland peaks and coastal promontories are being symbolically transformed into the tomb plan, the horns, facade, passages and chambers. Pentre Ifan, for example, has horns and facade, which are on an east/west axis—the same direction as the lower part of the Afon Nyfer. Similarly, the Bedd-yr-Afanc gallery grave is aligned along the centre of a large inland U-shaped valley. Similar localised orientations are present elsewhere. It would appear that the elongated shape of the tomb replicates river/valley direction.

The most complex (inner) architecture belongs to Cerrig y Gof. Here, passages and chambers are organised in a circular arrangement and point towards various upland and coastal features within the locality to the north and east, in particular the northern extent of Dinas Head and the western peaks and upland plateau of Mynydd Carningli. The tomb acts as a central point within the landscape and, although its plan has no orientation, there is a widening along the north-west/south-east axis. The five chambers, each possibly served by a small entrance, are aligned so as to ignore the rising and setting sun. The deposition of bone, assuming excarnation was practised, would have been periodic and may have played an important part in the life-cycle of those using the tomb. The existence of a social space created by the mechanical form of the chambers would not have detracted from the outer, organic appearance of the monument, the cairn or earthen mound merging with the landscape. Cerrig-y-Gof and other monuments within the group cannot therefore be said to dominate the landscape. They are merely part of it. We suggest a similar pattern recurs elsewhere within the area.

The unorthodox architecture of the Morfa Bycham tombs suggests a more pronounced attempt to encapsulate the landscape. Whilst two of these tombs apparently possessed no covering mound, all four monuments, located within a dense limestone rock outcrop, merge unseen into the landscape, as if purposely hidden. All are constructed of large, locally-cut angular blocks which have been placed over loosely-constructed chambers. Although we have argued that the outer part of the tomb is organic and the chamber area and passage inorganic, it would appear all four tombs represent quite the reverse. The immediate surroundings are of extensive rock outcropping and the tombs are constructed so as to be hidden, thus restricting the visual impact upon neighbouring groups or certain members of society.

Lost Monuments (see Appendix B)

One aspect that has not yet been covered in any detail is that of damaged, doubtful and lost monuments. Barker (1992) recognised 27 in total, the same number noted on the County Sites and Monuments Record. Of the 27 sites, ten still have visible evidence in the form of large, recumbent capstones and uprights or, in one case, an elongated mound (Morfa Bycham, SM 2213 0751). Of the remaining 17, little or nothing remains and these are known only as a result of antiquarian visits prior to their destruction. It is interesting to note that, if incorporated within the main list, these monuments would increase numbers within groups by 40%. Four areas stand out as being particularly dense. The Sites and Monuments Record, Barker (1992), Daniel (1950) and Grimes (1936) recognise an additional six monuments around the St David's peninsula. One,

Lower Trginnis (SM 7180 2360), was probably another earth-fast monument surrounded by a small cairn. The others, which are now lost, have been termed cromlechs. Three additional monuments are also noted in the Newport area. The two lost monuments are termed 'byrial chamber' and 'ruined cromlech'. The remains of the former, known as Trefoel (SM 1030 4030), has a cupmarked stone. A third monument, Carn Menyn (SM 1404 3262), is a round cairn with a capstone and three uprights and may be of the same generic group as Cerrig y Gof, west of Newport. However, it should be noted that no archaeological excavation has taken place at this site.

Four lost monuments are present within the Fishguard group, Coatan Arthur (SM 683 617), Glyn y Mel (SM 966 369), Man y Gromlech (SM 909 389) and Y Garn (SM 9142 3911).

But by far the largest group of lost monuments is located around the Pembroke area. Of these, four clusters are still visible in the form of uprights with, in one case, The Cuckoo Stones at Carew, the addition of a capstone.

Finally, the single monument in north Pembrokeshire, Cerrig Llwydion, was accompanied by a large cist structure known as Yr Hen Llech (SM 4128 3602), which still has visible remains of a capstone and single upright. Other possible monuments are located around this area, but are only mentioned in the Sites and Monuments Record. It is probable that this cluster was once as large and dense as some of the coastal groups.

These 27 monuments, plus the 37 discussed in the text, suggest that within south-west Wales, or more precisely the coastal areas of south-west Wales, a number of small territorial groups flourished. It is interesting to note that the majority of damaged and lost monuments occur within the spatial groups identified by the authors.

Different Places, Different Spaces: changes in symbolism
Towards the end of the Neolithic a series of monuments appear that neither truly represent the Neolithic nor fully anticipate the succeeding Bronze Age. These are standing stones and stone circles. It has been argued by some that stone circles are prehistoric observatories, each stone, each access point, representing a particular sunrise within the seasons. However, the authors (1996: 18-20) have suggested an alternative use. Standing stones, too, have in the past

received much comment, interpretations ranging from territorial markers to back scratchers for cattle!

South-west Wales is able to boast a large number of standing stones, as well as a henge monument and a stone circle. Many of the standing stones appear in groups of two, three or more. Single stones may, at one time, have been accompanied by more stones close by. Indeed, we would argue that we are only witnessing part of an extensive ritual landscape marking the transition between the Neolithic and the Early Bronze Age. Importantly, monuments of both periods use death as a focus for ritual activity. The henge, Meini Gwyr, (SN 142 266) has been interpreted by Houlder (1978, 178) as the remains of a large cairn circle. Now partially destroyed, Meini Gwyr stands on a broad ridge which may have been part of the route used to transport the Stonehenge bluestones. Only two of the 17 stones that once formed the embanked circle survive. Excavations in 1985-86 revealed a passageway on the western section of the circle. This may have a symbolic association with the rising and setting of the sun. Close by, to the north and south of Meini Gwyr, are two tumuli and the remains of a burial chamber, suggesting the existence of a ritual landscape. In keeping with the pattern found elsewhere, the tumuli and Meini Gwyr are on low, flat land, whereas the chambered monument to the north (SN 1382 2660) stands on a small ridge. Approximately 2.5km to the north is the Gors Fawr stone circle, part of a complex which also includes two standing stones located 200m to the north on a flat plateau of marsh upland pasture. A series of cairns is located high on the Preseli Mountains to the north and east and all are clearly intervisible with the stone circle. The circle itself is now reduced to 16 upright stones, the remainder being either recumbent or missing. None is above a metre high and all are spaced between 2.5m and 5m apart, within a diameter of 22m. Unlike the Meini Gwyr monument, there is no bank or ditch. Houlder (1978, 184) has suggested the two standing stones to the north-east are related outliers. Traditionalists might suggest these act as astronomical markers for measuring the sun's winter solstice. However, the authors have suggested a completely different interpretation (1996, 61), that monuments such as Gors Fawr are in fact symbolically and ritually controlled within the act of initiation, rebirth and death. The linearity of the stone circle, the standing stones and the cairns suggests a 'path', a processional route, the cairns clearly representing a final resting place—journey's end. The stone circle, therefore, may represent the beginning of that death—a space where the dead could be viewed, a form of 'lying in state' before interment. Within the circle, the space is special and sacred and very different from that directly outside and downslope. These markers within the landscape would, therefore, signify a spatial as well as a chronological journey into the afterlife. The Gors Fawr complex may also have been used for rituals of rebirth, a notion inextricably linked with death. It will be recalled that the upland clans of Madagascar wrap the deceased in a ceremonial cloth which, when the body is exhumed some years later, is used by relatives for copulation. Stone circle complexes such as Gors Fawr may have been the site of similar rituals, in which the dead and the living become one.

Although in active use within a fairly narrow time frame, these monuments have never ceased to exert an influence. Whilst many standing stones are located on isolated, undulating or non-productive pasture, others are found close to roads or field boundaries, suggesting that when these were under construction standing stones were considered important markers. Indeed, we have argued (1994) that many Herefordshire standing stones were used to delineate parish boundaries.

One particular cluster of interest is the stone alignment of Parc y Meirw (Field of the Dead). This megalithic alignment, the longest in Wales, once consisted of eight stones but only four now stand. The alignment is 40m long and orientated north-west/south-east. It runs along the line of a small country road between Tre-llan and Trellwyn (3km south-east of Fishguard) (SM 998 358), the tallest stone standing about 2.5m high. Further west, located a few hundred metres from Haven Point and 3km west of the Nab Head is Skomer Island. The majority of monuments on the island are of Iron Age date. However, Evans (1986, 3) has suggested that the Harold Stone (SM 7345 0957), to the north-east of two large Iron Age settlements and related field systems, may be of Late Neolithic date. Scattered around the island also are seven clusters of cairns, which may be the result of field clearances but, alternatively, may have been used for Bronze Age burials.

Concluding Remarks: landscape as artefact

Throughout this chapter, we have emphasised the importance of a Neolithic structured on the following criteria:

Firstly, the Neolithic, and more to the point, the building of megalithic monuments, was a slow ongoing process that had its origins firmly rooted in the Mesolithic. There was a need to establish an identity based upon ancestry. This, above all, created a history and a sense of belonging. This sense of belonging is formulated on the visuality of landscape; the process of perception and familiarity.

Secondly, the location of the 37 monuments conforms to a number of structured rules. The spatial distribution of all monuments is such that a number of definite clusters has been recognised. Within each cluster, tombs are sited either on the peripheries (and some way inland) or close to the coast. Orientation of both the chamber and mound is localised and, in our opinion, points to—or at least acknowledges—various landscape forms and the sea. All but one group (the Inland Pembrokeshire Group) are located around large coastal peninsula and estuarine environs. In addition, and adopting Richard Bradley's idea of monuments becoming 'places', each tomb may have been built close to, or on, pathways used by the Mesolithic ancestors of Neolithic communities.

Thirdly, nearly all the monuments have, at some time, been excavated, in many cases badly. The finds, although few, do suggest that they were used by high-status groups. Evidence of imported prestige polished flint and stone axes bears witness to this. In addition to artefacts, cremated human remains from at least 15% of the monuments reveal a society bound up in ritual-symbolic burial activity. However, many tombs in this region were plundered by antiquarians during the early part of this and in preceding centuries. Compounding this difficulty, many of the monuments are located on acidic soils, which, over time, would have dissolved any bone material contained within the chambers.

Time for monument building and burial must have been just as important as the day-to-day organisation of society. Tilley (1994) has concluded that monuments in this area were possibly not used for 'successive interment'. Elsewhere, the evidence for burial deposition and use suggests that monuments underwent several phases of abandonment during the later Neolithic and Early Bronze Age.

Each monument may have fulfilled a primary role as a meeting place along a known path or trackway. Burial may have been secondary to this original conception. The evidence indicates, especially from a number of 'earth fast' tombs, that cremated bone deposition is stratified suggesting continual use, albeit periodic. This being the case, each monument fulfils two major roles; one as a landscape marker, the other to inter the dead. In the succeeding chapters, points raised here will be considered in relation to each of the south-west Wales monuments.

The Newport Group

The Newport Group (Landranger 145) comprises six monuments—
Bedd-yr-Afanc, Pentre Ifan, Cerrig y Gof, Carreg Coetan,
Trellyffant and Llech-y-Tribedd—which encompass an area of
around 40km². Other monuments may have existed, but due to
intensive agricultural activity over recent centuries are now long
gone. The area has a continuous early prehistory dating back at
least to 6,000 BC. Flint from the Late Mesolithic has been found all
along the mud flats of the Afon Nyfer (Nevern) estuary. Between
the estuary, the coast and the mountains, Neolithic mortuary structures occupy the intermediate slopes. Above these slopes, and all
along the northern extent of the Mynydd Preseli overlooking
Newport, Bronze Age and Iron Age activity is also represented.

Domestic life for Neolithic communities in around the Afon
Nyfer valley seems to have been rather favourable. A choice of
economic resources would have been available, ranging from
coastal and riverine fishing and hunting/gathering to limited animal
husbandry and crop cultivation. This suggests the transition from
the Mesolithic to the Neolithic in this area did not occur
'overnight'. The area within the estuary would have been lightly
wooded and foraged by large mammals such as red and roe deer.
Samples of wood discovered within the inter-tidal peats of the Afon
Nyfer estuary (-0.6m O.D.)[1] have been dated to about 5,100 BC,
confirming the environment in and around Newport was wooded.
Indeed, this and similar samples from Cardigan Bay, form part of a
submerged forest.

---

1. O.D. stands for Ordnance Datum, the mean of high and low tide

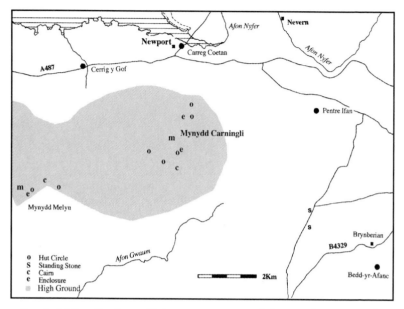

Spatial Distribution of Monuments around the northern Preselis

For each of the tombs in this cluster, the primary landscape focus seems to be the rocky outcrop of Mynydd Carningli, at the north-easterly extent of the Mynydd Preseli. Three of the monuments—Pentre Ifan, Carreg Coetan and Llech-y-Tribedd—all have capstones that appear to replicate the summit of the outcrop, drawing the landscape within the architecture of the tomb. It must be stressed, however, that what we see today is only the tomb 'skeleton'. During the Neolithic, this skeleton would have possessed 'flesh'—a covering earthen mound—although in each case, the capstone may have been partly exposed in order to emphasise the symbolic association with Carningli. Apart from the gallery grave of Bedd-yr-Afanc, which probably dates from the latest phase of the Neolithic, the remaining Newport tombs—despite their damaged and, in some cases ruined, state—probably also embody a process of replication and control which seeks to establish and perpetuate a sense of identity between the group and its landscape. Tombs belonging to clusters elsewhere in south-west Wales tend to confirm these observations, revealing a similar pattern of landscape orientation. The chamber at St Elvis Farm, St David's, for example, is angled down towards a small coastal valley, an inlet of the River Solva.

However, given this general association with Carningli, individual monuments of the Newport Group are nevertheless sited within diverse landscape settings, ranging from coastal locations to inland valley floor sites. Apart from Cerrig y Gof and perhaps Carreg Coetan, tombs appear to ignore the draw of the sea. Indeed, the two monuments of Llech-y-Tribedd and Trellyffant, although only 0.5km from the coast, appear to be deliberately hidden from the sea. Both are on south-facing ridges overlooking the Mynydd Preseli. This pattern recurs throughout the south-west Wales peninsula.

Due to the diversity of architectural forms, the dating of individual tombs is difficult. We cannot say with certainty that all the tombs in this group were constructed about the same time. However, they were probably all in use during the middle and later phases of the Neolithic. It has been suggested that simple 'portal dolmens', such as Carreg Coetan, are the earliest monuments in this area. This type of monument probably functioned as a simple tomb incorporating a small chamber which housed a single burial, probably that of an important figure in Early Neolithic society. Following this burial event, the tomb may have continued to function as a significant place within the landscape, changing its symbolic significance through time. Indeed, towards the latter part of the Neolithic and the Early Bronze Age there is evidence for monuments in this area becoming political statements within the landscape—their identity changing, but not their form. For instance, at Trellyffant, the tomb has ceased to be a monument for the dead. The 35 cupmarks on the capstone, possibly Bronze Age in date, indicate a transformation of the ideology associated with the tomb. It is suggested that these cupmarks act as a rejection of the old (Neolithic) order (Children and Nash, 1994). The equivalent can be seen today, with redundant chapels being reused as workshops and dwellings. Here, the building has changed its meaning, but not its architectural from.

Of the six monuments, Bedd-yr-Afanc stands out and has been classified as a Late Neolithic gallery grave. Its construction, location and orientation suggest a change in monument ideology. Located inland, and oriented east/west along the valley floor, the tomb ignores Carningli, the sea and other monuments. Elsewhere, gallery graves follow a similar pattern. Compared with earlier monuments, they are smaller, less intrusive and sometimes actually hidden. With its covering earthen mound, Bedd-yr-Afanc would have merged with the valley floor. Without specialist ritual knowledge, the tomb would have been invisible, with access restricted to members of the local group.

Looking west across the Nevern estuary at high tide

Bedd-yr-Afanc, Meline

> Only definite gallery grave in Wales
> Location: Near village of Brynberian, south-east of Newport
> (SN 1087 3457)
> Access: Across a raised bog!

From the village of Eglwyswrw go west along the A487. Approximately 1km down this road, take a left fork on the B4329 towards Henry's Moat. About 4km down this road, and just before the village of Brynberian, park on the left-hand side in front of an electricity sub-station. Backtrack for 10m or so to a small unmetalled track on the same side of the road. On the left, 20m from the track, is a gate opening out onto marshy land. Walk due south for approximately 400m. Extreme caution is needed when crossing this bog area. Furthermore, Bedd-yr-Afanc is very difficult to locate. However, looking back towards a barn roof and running one's eye due south from the roof to Cwmcerwyn, the monument should be clearly visible on a small rise, 20m or so from the Afon Brynberian.

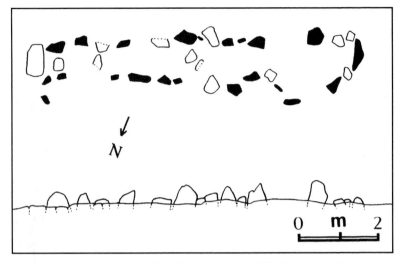

0   m   2

Located in the middle of a dramatic U-shaped valley, on a slightly raised plateau surrounded by marshland, close to Mynydd Preseli, Bedd-yr-Afanc is the only definite example of a gallery grave in Wales. Architecturally, it is quite different from its nearest neighbour, Pentre Ifan, which lies 3.8km to the north-west.

Lacking side chambers and forecourt, the tomb was originally covered by an oval barrow measuring approximately 21.3m by 8.2m and perhaps 1.5m high (Royal Commission for Ancient Monuments—RCAM). The tomb itself consists of 22 small orthostats (upright stones) arranged to form a gallery 10.5m long and 2.5m wide, orientated roughly east-west. The gallery is blocked at the western end. The orientation of the tomb may be governed by the east-west alignment of the rising and setting sun, as well as symbolising the life and death cycle; the west being the termination of life and the setting of the sun.

The tomb was excavated in 1938 by Grimes, who noted traces of two lines of stones, possibly defining the extent of the mound. The tomb is sited on an exposed (raised) ancient land surface. Conspicuous within the immediate landscape yet 'invisible' within the wider local landscape, it sits at the centre of a small, rather inaccessible, island. It is difficult to assess the type of vegetation that surrounded this island when the monument was in use. However, pollen analysis may suggest an environment similar to that of the

Bedd-yr-Afanc looking south

present day. This would mean that the extensive valley floor marsh-land was probably the result of periglacial activity, rather than of climatic deterioration during the Late Bronze Age. The peripheries of this classic U-shaped valley were probably covered by extensive broad-leaved woodland, similar to that within the neighbouring Nevern Valley. The tomb is orientated along the marshy valley, the location suggesting an intimate affinity with topographic features to either side, especially Cnwc-yr-Hydd, Cerrig Lladron and mountains to the south. During the Neolithic, the tomb may have been surrounded by seasonal water-logging. This would have set up both a physical and mental barrier, maintaining the exclusivity of the site and safely containing the dead within the confines of the tomb and the raised plateau on which it stood. Settlement would probably have been confined to the intermediate slopes, away from the damp valley floor.

Pentre Ifan, Nevern

Impressive terminally-chambered long cairn with forecourt
Location: 4km east of Newport (SN 0994 3707)
Access: Public footpath from lay-by

From Newport, head east along the A487. Take the second turning on the right-hand side, signposted 'Pentre Ifan'. About 0.5km from the hamlet of Sychpant, turn left and follow the sign to Pentre Ifan for 1km. Take the third right and after about 0.75km park in a lay-by on the left. The monument is reached about 200m along a footpath which leads off opposite the lay-by.

One of the most famous of South Wales' chambered tombs, Pentre Ifan consists of a tilted capstone, dipping towards the Afon Nyfer valley to the north, perched upon three tall upright megaliths or orthostats. The resulting chamber is 3m long, 2m wide and 3m high. The chamber was originally cut about 40cms into the ground surface and lined with drystone walling, but has recently been infilled. The blocking stone (doorway) in the forecourt area was packed with small stones around the base. On the outer face of the blocking stone, a single cupmark and ring has been identified (Lynch, 1974, 120), although we failed to recognise such regular patterning.

The tomb is an impressive example of a terminally-chambered long cairn with a semicircular forecourt set in the broad southern end of the barrow—a model Closed Portal Tomb. Daniel compares the forecourt at Pentre Ifan and other chambered tombs in the region with the so-called 'horned cairns' of Carlingford in Ireland, arguing for colonisation by people of the Carlingford culture. He further suggests that the more easterly Severn-Cotswold tomb group is derived from the Pentre Ifan type. Lynch (1972) has suggested the tomb was built in two phases. Phase one may have consisted only of the chamber, uprights and capstone with a low square cairn. Phase two would have seen the construction of a low mound, perhaps with the capstone left exposed.

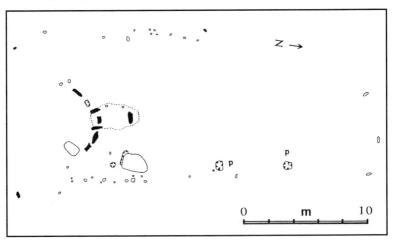

Pentre Ifan, Nevern—note the extent of the kerbing and possible earlier ritual pits (p)

Grimes, who excavated the tomb in 1936/37 and again in 1958/59 for the Office of Works, described the forecourt, where ritual feasts may have been held, as consisting of two orthostats placed either side of an entrance, itself blocked by a massive upright. Hemp argued that blocked chambers, found also at Capel Garmon and Dyffryn Ardudwy, prevented tombs being fully re-opened after the mound had been piled up (Hemp, 1927). His belief led him to propose the theory that tombs were constructed to house the remains of 'great chieftains', and that the other individuals found in the chambers had, in life, been relatives or attendants who had sacrificed themselves on the death of the great man. The chambers would therefore have been used once only by high-ranking members of a stratified society and would not have been intended for communal use. Daniel, however, argued that 'chamber tombs were for the most part used collectively on a number of occasions' (1950). This is interesting in that the doorway is firmly set into the ground. We suggest that this doorway was opened only on special occasions, and, rather than fresh bodies being placed into the tomb, collections of bones were stored up elsewhere before being deposited en masse in the chamber. This hypothesis challenges Barker's idea (1992) that the doorway was a permanent feature, a false portal, similar to those of the hybrid Severn-Cotswold tombs such as Ty Isaf and Pipton Long Cairn in the Black Mountains.

The mound itself does not survive, but may originally have measured 40m long and 17m wide. Traces of possible stone kerbing have been identified delineating the long sides of the barrow. However, the alignments of these stones do not match precisely the orientation of the barrow and they may be linked instead with possible ritual pits found beneath the mound and predating its construction. Pentre Ifan, which is intervisible with Carreg Coetan and Llech-y-Tribedd, yielded a small number of flint flakes and fragments of Welsh (Western) pottery. These are similar to examples from the excavated chambered monument of Pant-y-Saer, North Wales. Grimes distinguishes between the pottery of the western megalithic groups, with its 'flattened, expanded hammer-head rims' and that of the south and east of England. Lynch (1969) has noted similarities of form, but not of fabric, between the neck of an open bowl discovered in the chamber at Pentre Ifan and fragments recovered from Dyffryn Ardudwy in Gwynedd.

Note the dip of the capstone and the slope of Carningli—both point to the sea and the Afon Nyfer valley

Cerrig y Gof, Newport

Possible transitional tomb to Bronze Age
Location: 8km east of Fishguard (SM 0365 3890)
Access: Lies alongside A487

Take the A487 from Newport towards Fishguard. About 2km from
Newport park on the right-hand side of the A487, just before the track
to Holmhouse Isaf. The tomb lies just a few metres from the road and
is clearly visible. This monument is also accessible from the
Pembrokeshire coastal path, about 0.75km above Aber Rhigian.

Also known as Cerrig Atgof, this unusual coastal tomb stands
between Dinas Head and the Afon Nyfer. Affinities with tombs in
Ireland and Scotland have been noted, and it has been suggested
that architectural influences were transmitted along Irish Sea trade
routes (Castleden, 1992). Daniel (1950) includes the tomb within
his Irish Sea cultural province as a late innovation of the local
Pembrokeshire group.

The tomb is possibly transitional, suggesting Bronze Age burial
practice in its use of multiple cists, or small stone-lined burial
chambers, within an oval mound. Close by and to the south of
Cerrig y Gof is arguably a dense Bronze Age landscape consisting

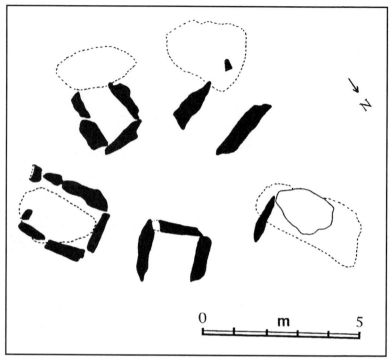

*Cerrig y Gof, Newport. This tomb possibly encompasses promi-
nent features within the surrounding landscape. It may be
divorced from other tombs within the Newport Group. The
central area of Cerrig y Gof (as in the photograph on the previous
page), looks out towards Dinas Head, an area of intense
Mesolithic activity*

of cairns, hut circles and enclosures. Furthermore, a possible
Bronze Age hillfort, one of only two in Wales, is sited on Carningli.

The mound measures 9m north-south and 8.2m east-west, and
contains five square and rectangular chambers lacking passages.

Cerrig y Gof was excavated in 1811 by Fenton, who discovered
'charcoal, and soon after pieces of urns of the rudest pottery, some
particles of bones and a quantity of black sea pebbles'. He believed
a central cromlech originally completed the complex. This argument is disputed because the central area is too small to accommodate a chamber of a size similar to the other five.

A confusion of stone: three of the five chambers at Cerrig y Gof

Certain prominent topographical features in the surrounding landscape seem to be acknowledged by the tomb. The north-west chamber acknowledges Dinas Head and Newport Bay; the south-west, Mynydd Dinas; the south-east, Mynydd Melyn; and the eastern chamber, Carningli. All of these areas have yielded evidence of intense Bronze Age activity. By indicating significant features, Cerrig y Gof is encompassing the landscape. We disagree with the idea put forward by Lynch (1972) that the chamber settings are 'a haphazard agglomeration which must be the local answer to the need for more burial space within a tradition of single compartment monuments'. On the contrary, each chamber appears to be deliberately positioned to achieve an overall symmetry. Furthermore, each chamber may not have housed just one body. Each could have contained many bones, not necessarily from one skeleton, but from a number. Whole families may, over many generations, have been deposited as disarticulated remains or even as cremations.

Carreg Coetan, Newport

Tripod Dolmen
Location: On the estuary in Newport (SN 0602 3935)
Access: By public footpath

From the centre of Newport, head towards Cardigan. Take the left turning signposted 'Treath' (beach). Follow this road for approximately 200m. On the left-hand side there is a small unmetalled road leading to a group of bungalows. Carreg Coetan is clearly signposted from the main road. The monument is located about 30m from the turning between two bungalows.

Also known as Coetan Arthur (Arthur's Quoit), this so-called 'tripod dolmen' consists in fact of four uprights, two of which support a massive sloping capstone. A number of outlying stones belonging to the tomb have been identified, together with traces of a covering mound. In between the uprights is a small rectangular or polygonal chamber. Littered within the vicinity and concentrated

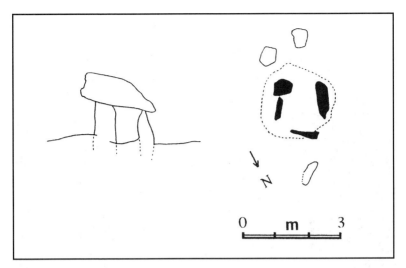

about 2m in front of the chamber is possible evidence of blocking material. During the 1979/80 excavation carried out by Sian Rees (1981), it became evident that a build-up of plough soil, in places over a metre thick, lay around the uprights. This being so, Carreg Coetan would originally have appeared much taller than it does today.

One of the lowest-lying tombs in Wales, Carreg Coetan stands just 8m above sea-level close to the Afon Nyfer estuary and 0.5km from the coast. The estuary and Dinas Head lie to the west; while to the south, and rising to a height of 350m, the summit of Carningli provides the obvious topographical focal point for the tomb and was probably a focus for ritual, if not social and economic activity. Although the remains of human activity on Carningli indicate either a Bronze Age or early Iron Age hillfort, this prominent feature would, by its sheer monumental presence within the landscape, surely also have attracted Neolithic communities. Indeed, legend states that the stones forming Carreg Coetan were thrown from the summit of the mountain. Furthermore, if we accept that human activity is continuous through time, it could be argued that Mesolithic hunter-gatherers also utilised the slopes of this impressive natural monument. When aligned with the peak, the capstone appears to replicate its profile, drawing the landscape into the fabric of the tomb.

Cairn works along the northern slopes of Carningli,
probably Bronze Age in date

The much disturbed chamber, when recently excavated, revealed traces of 'powdery, cremated bone' along with two sherds of corded Beaker and three rim-sherds of Grooved Ware. Large amounts of pottery, enough for two pot reconstructions, and more cremated bone lay deeper within the chamber stratigraphy. Charcoal beneath an upright socket was carbon-dated to about 2700 BC. The fact that both cremated bone and charcoal are present in the chamber suggests that bodies were not deposited in the tomb immediately after death. A more elaborate burial method may have been used. We tend to favour the idea that prior to cremation the dead were exposed to the elements, possibly on wooden platforms like those used by the North West American coastal Indians. Here, the body would decay, the flesh devoured by wild animals, to leave only a skeleton that could no longer be recognised as human.

Trellyffant, Nevern

Double chambered tomb
Location: between Newport and Molygrove (SN 0822 4252)
Access: Permission needed from Trellyffant farm

From the village of Moylgrove, take the road leading south-west to Newport Beach (and golf course). The third turn to the left leads to Trellyffant farm and permission to visit the tomb, which lies on private land, should be sought at the farmhouse. Trellyfant is also referred to as Trellyfaint or Trellefan.

Powell (*et. al.*, 1969) defines Trellyffant, a ruined chambered tomb, as a portal dolmen. Originally, the chamber seems to have been rectangular, and Daniel, writing in the 1950s, gave a height of 1.8m, with an opening to the south-east. The capstone appears to have been oriented north-west/south-east, measuring 2.1m by 1.8m, and there are traces of a covering mound. To the north of the main chamber is a small square feature—possibly another chamber, making Trellyfant a double chambered tomb. Lynch (1972) suggests that a cairn or earthen mound would originally have covered both chambers.

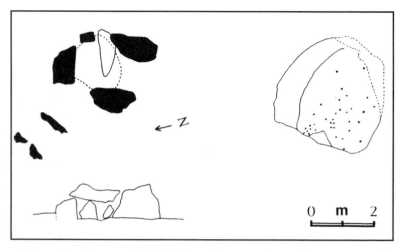

Plan, elevation and distribution of cupmarks on the capstone of the Trellyffant monument

The existence of a possible second chamber is unusual. Although double chambers are frequent around the North Wales coast—they are found at Dyffryn Ardudwy (NGR SH 588 229), for example, and at Trefignath, on Anglesey (NGR SH 259 805)—the architectural form is rare in this part of Wales. A possible entrance to the monument is located to the west. A recumbent stone lies between two uprights at the eastern side of the existing chamber.

There is evidence of later prehistoric ritual defacement of a Neolithic chambered tomb on the upper surface of the capstone at Trellyffant. The 35 cupmarks identified on the stone may be of Bronze Age origin and associated with the appropriation and re-use of the tomb by people seeking to alter its meaning, perhaps transforming what was once principally a mortuary structure into a monument marking the site of exchange transactions or political gatherings. Such acts may be interpreted as attempts to subvert remote and irrelevant beliefs. The authenticity of the Trellyffant cupmarks, however, has been questioned. The Welsh Commission on Ancient Monuments has argued that, owing to the random size and distribution of the marks, they should be regarded as natural. Daniel, however, believes the cupmarks to be genuine and some of the finest in southern Britain.

The Trellyffant monument showing both chambers

About 3km to the south-east of Trellyffant burial chamber further cupmarks are visible on a rock[2], which Daniel believed was the capstone of a destroyed megalithic chamber, but which is probably natural. Cupmarks are one of several megalithic art forms found in Wales. Others include concentric circles, zig-zags, multiple lines and human designs, but these are confined to two passage graves on Anglesey: Bryn Celli Ddu and Barclodiad-y-Gawres.

As a footnote, the medieval Welsh historian and geographer, Giraldus Cambrensis (Gerald of Wales), believed that Trellyffant ('Toad's Hall') was so named because a chieftain buried inside the tomb had been devoured by toads.

---

2. The site of Trefael, Nevern (SN 1030 4030) has at least 28 cupmarks, 17 of these are shallow depressions. Locating these cupmarks is difficult due to lichen encroachment. Lynch (1972, 79) suggests this may well be the capstone of a destroyed burial monument. Further cupmarks may well exist beneath the present turf-line.

Llech-y-Tribedd, Moylgrove

Capstone supported on three orthostats
Location: Between Newport and Moylgrove (SN 1005 4319)
Access: Permission needed from Penlan Farm

From the village of Moylgrove, proceed south-west along a wide country lane towards Newport beach (and golf course). Take the second left up an unmetalled road, signposted 'Penlan Farm'. Llech-y-Tribedd is sited in a small field approximately 700m up this narrow, rough track. The tomb is clearly visible from the track. Access is via a stile. Permission is required from Penlan Farm before visiting this monument.

The tomb comprises a single large capstone supported by three uprights, and the chamber appears to be similar in size and plan to nearby Trellyfant. The uprights are arranged in a tripod form; another is located close by suggesting the chamber was once rectangular. In 1693, it was reported that this fourth upright was in place and supported the capstone. Legend has it that St Samson originally threw the stones for the monument from the summit of

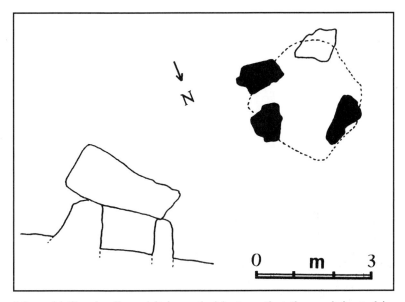

Mynydd Carningli, and it is probably true that they originated in the Mynydd Preseli. A spread of rubble within the chamber area may be the remains of an extensive cairn, possibly oriented east/west. Stone from the cairn has probably been used in the construction of a number of earthen boundaries that surround the monument.

The monument (also referred to as the Altar Stone, Llech-y-Drybedd and Samson's Quoit) commands one of the most outstanding views of any tomb in the area, and draws in the whole extent of the north Mynydd Preseli. The triangular capstone points towards Mynydd Carningli, a focal point for nearly all the tombs in this area. Indeed, the south-eastern point of the capstone appears to replicate its summit. By contrast, Llech-y-Tribedd is completely hidden from the sea, although located on a south-east facing ridge, only 0.6km from the coast (see photograph over-leaf). Ignoring the 'visuality' of the sea appears to be a common trait among monuments within this part of Wales. Others, especially those along the south Pembrokeshire coast, appear to be similarly sited. These, however, unlike Llech-y-Tribedd, can be classified as earth-fast monuments (e.g. St Elvis' Farm, the Garn Wen group and the Devil's Quoit, Angle). This monument,

Above: Llech-y-Tribedd looking south—the sea is not in view
Below: Looking east

although probably associated with marine economies, is aligned to inland landscape features.

The Fishguard Group

This group (Landranger 157) consists of ten monuments—Carreg Samson, Parc-y-Garn, Ffyst Samson, Ffynnondruidion, Gyllwch/Garn Gilfach, Garn Wen (3 monuments), Parc-y-Cromlech and Carn Wnda. With the exception of Carreg Samson, all are small, hidden, unobtrusive monuments. The group itself, like others within south-west Wales, is architecturally diverse. Around Fishguard there is a series of so-called 'earth fast' monuments. To the south, the classic dolmen type predominates, whereas several monuments within the central uplands of Strumble Head conform to neither the dolmen nor the 'earth fast' classification.

At least seven of these tombs may be considered 'earth fast'— Garn Wen (3), Carn Wnda, Garn Gilfach, Parc-y-Garn and Ffynnondruidion. Tombs of this type have one end of the capstone deliberately placed on the edge of an earth-cut pit, rather than being supported by upright stones. They are also sited on the intermediate slopes, among extensive rock outcropping. It is suggested that they were never totally covered by an earthen mound. Daniel (1950) believes a shallow cairn may have been banked up against the side of the chamber in order to conceal the burial. This being the case, each tomb would have merged with the surrounding rocky land-scape, users relying on local ritual knowledge in order to locate it.

All the 'earth fast' tombs concentrated to the north of the distrib-ution take the sea as their main visual focus, even though each is locally orientated. The dramatic landscape of St David's Head to the west is an important focal point for the five southernmost tombs.

This series of monuments appears to be divided topographically into two distinct groups: lowland and upland. The largest tomb in

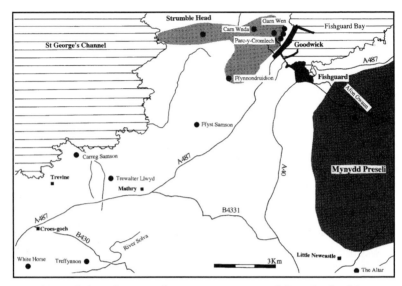

Spatial distribution of monuments in north Pembrokeshire

the Fishguard Group is Carreg Samson, which is similar in size to nearby Pentre Ifan. Its landscape setting is also comparable, as the monument looks towards the fertile lowlands and sea beyond, while acknowledging the jagged rocky outcropping along Garn Fawr, Garn Gilfach and Garn Wnda to the north-east.

The architectural variety of the Fishguard group of monuments suggests that they were constructed at different times during the Neolithic. The 'earth fast' monuments are probably later than the other types, perhaps dating to the Neolithic/Bronze Age transition. This assumption is based purely on burial deposition, as no carbon dating evidence is available.

58

Carreg Samson, Mathry

An impressive megalithic tomb
Location: Near the village of Trevine, on the coast roughly
mid-way between St David's and Fishguard (SM 8483 3350)
Access: Lies adjacent to a public footpath
from which it can be seen

Carreg Samson is one of south-west Wales' most impressive mega-lithic tombs, second only to Pentre Ifan. From the village of Mathry on the A487, roughly halfway between Fishguard and St David's, head west towards St David's. At the Square and Compass Inn, turn right, following the signpost to Trevine. At Trevine turn right down a narrow country lane signposted 'Abercastle'. Approximately 1.2km down this road, take the first left, signposted 'Longhouse Farm'. Carreg Samson is located 300m north-east of the main farm buildings, adjacent to a narrow farm track, a few metres off a public footpath.

This monument was once known as the grave of Samson's finger. It was held that St Samson, believed to be a son of a 6th century royal courtier who went on to become abbot of the

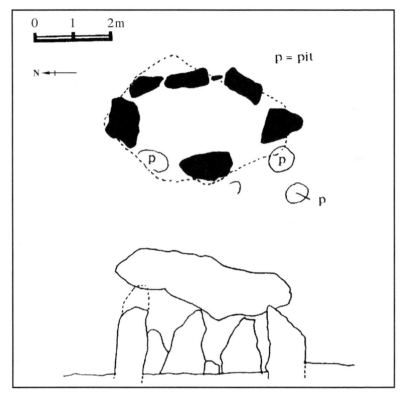

Plan and elevation. Note also related pits (p)
Strumble Head can be seen in the background of the photograph

monastery of Piro on Caldey Island, lifted the capstone into place with his little finger.

The capstone dips towards the immediate bay and Strumble Head beyond. To the east and north-east, the landscape is dominated by the jagged peaks of Garn Fawr, Garn Gilfach and Garn Wnda. On all three peaks there is evidence of Neolithic ritual. To the south, another two tombs stand close by: White Horse and Treffynnon. Hidden from view to the west are the jagged peaks of Carn Llidi, Carnedd-lleithr, Carn-ffald and St David's Head. The monument, on a north-facing slope, is not sited on the highest point.

Carreg Samson, also known as Carrig Samson, or The Longhouse, was excavated by Frances Lynch in 1968. It is constructed from an enormous capstone (5.3m by 3.6m) supported by three of the seven large uprights to form an oval/polygonal chamber (3.3m by 1.7m). Both the uprights and chamber have been constructed over an irregularly-cut pit. The elongated shape of the chamber and capstone suggest that there was once a large rectangular covering mound, possibly comparable in size to nearby Pentre Ifan. However, no direct evidence for a mound or cairn survives.

Excavation has shown that the entrance was located in the northwestern part of the chamber, with an approximately 2m-long passage leading from it. A pit was formed around the uprights, as at Pentre Ifan. During the recent past, the chamber has been used as a sheep shelter and some investigators have recorded drystone walling or packing between the uprights. The authors were not able to verify this when visiting the site in 1992 and 1996, although there were a large number of stones littering the floor of the chamber.

The finds from the chamber were few, but did include fragments of burnt bone. Outside, a pot dating to the Early Neolithic was recovered (Lynch, 1976, 75). Furthermore, the discovery of three pits, two within the chamber area, the other a metre to the southeast, suggests evidence of ritual activity prior to construction of the monument as the pits are located where the fabric of the cairn would have been during the Neolithic. This is not an uncommon finding. For example, extensive pre-monument activity, in the form of a lithic scatter dating to the Upper Palaeolithic, together with post holes, has been identified at the Neolithic monument of Gwernvale, in the Black Mountains. Similarly, Carreg Samson may have been the site of earlier prehistoric activity.

Trewalter Llwyd, Mathry

A capstone and single orthostat
Location: Near the village of Mathry, roughly mid-way between
St David's and Fishguard on the A487 (SM 8682 3176)
Access: On a public footpath

From the village of Mathry, roughly half-way along the A487
between Fishguard and St David's, proceed west along the A487 for
approximately 1km. Take the first right turning to Parc-y-Garn
Farm (down an unmetalled farm track). From the farm, walk east
along a public footpath. Trewalter Llwyd (also referred to as the
Walter Llwyd Dolmen and Parc-y-Garn) is incorporated into a field
boundary wall, 400m from the farm. The monument is clearly
visible from the south.

The tomb comprises a large single capstone (4.1m by 2.5m) and
one visible collapsed upright. Other uprights may well exist
beneath the boundary wall structure. Now much damaged,
Trewalter Llwyd would, in earlier times, have looked very much
like Llech-y-Tribedd or the White Horse tomb. In other words, a
tomb of true monumentality. It appears to form part of a group that

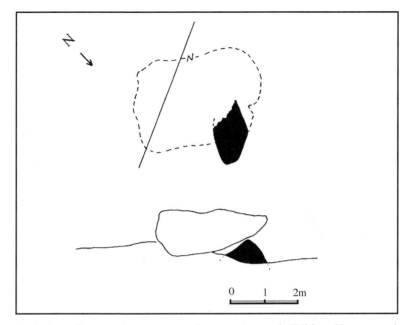

includes Carreg Samson to the north, and White Horse and Treffynnon to the west. All four tombs may delineate the inland extent of a territory. It was reported by Fenton in 1810, and later by Gardner Wilkinson in 1871, that at least one other tomb may have existed close by.

Trewalter Llwyd is sited within a slightly undulating landscape and, from the top of the capstone, the sea is visible approximately 4km away. It also shares intervisibility with Carreg Samson (also known as the Longhouse), 3km to the north-west. In the far distance, to the west and north-east, are the jagged peaks of St David's and Strumble Head.

It is worth noting that this monument, together with others such as Parc-y-llyn and The Altar, are incorporated into extensive earthen boundaries. This suggests that they remained significant monuments, important enough politically to be preserved within linear boundary features, rather than being destroyed.

Ffyst Samson, St Nicholas

A much damaged chambered tomb
Location: About 5km west of Fishguard (SM 9059 3492)
Access: Adjacent to a public footpath

This monument is sited on the large rock outcrop called Carn Llys. From the village of Mathry, proceed along the A487 towards Goodwick and Fishguard. About 3km along this road, take a left turning signposted 'St Nicholas'. Continue along this narrow country lane for approximately 1.5km, past a disused quarry on the right. Just before a farmhouse on the left is a public footpath off to the right. Walk along this for about 600m. The monument is located on a small, exposed, rocky plateau.

Ffyst Samson, also known as Trellys Cromlech, Trellysycoed, Ffst Samson and Samson's Quoit, is now much damaged. It comprises a single capstone supported by two enormous uprights, each standing to a height of well over a metre above the present ground surface. The original chamber may have been rectangular. Small stones litter the floor, both inside and outside the chamber indicating either the remnants of a cairn, or a stone-lined chamber.

Ffyst Samson looking south

There is evidence around the tomb of a slightly raised, and possibly circular mound (Barker, 1992).

Unlike other tombs in the locality, Ffyst Samson stands on a high point within the landscape. A few metres to the east, an exposed rock outcrop is visible from the site of the Ffynnondruidion monument. To the south-west, Ffyst Samson is intervisible with the monuments of Carreg Samson and Trewalter Llwyd, and is also within full view of the sea and St David's Head to the west. This monument may have been an important focal point given its location on such a dramatic rock outcrop. The mound would have been constructed of local stone to merge with the exposed rock outcropping close by. This tomb was therefore not a visual concept, but one constructed through ritual and symbolic knowledge. A similar idea can be put forward for Garn Gilfach, a few kilometres north of Ffyst Samson. To the east and beyond the small hill on which Ffyst Samson stands is a large standing stone and cairn, again suggesting continuity of use through time.

Ffynnondruidion, St Nicholas

> Destroyed
> Location: About 4km west of Fishguard (SM 9204 3679)
> Access: By permission from Ffynnon Druidion Farm

From the village of Mathry on the A487 take the turning left (if heading towards Fishguard) signposted 'St Nicholas'. Drive along this narrow country lane for about 5km, past a turning left to St Nicholas. Take the third right turning at Ffynnon Druidion Farm. The monument, now sadly destroyed, was sited within the farmyard, 30m past the main farm buildings on the right.

Daniel (1950) says only a few stones exist. Barber & Williams (1989) claim the monument was visible in 1985. However, a report from *Archaeologia Cambrensis* in 1872 (p.139) notes that the monument was entirely demolished, leaving just one or two stones to mark the site where the chamber once stood. Fifty years earlier Fenton noted that a burial chamber had once existed on the site. The remnants of a possible capstone and uprights are just visible in an overgrown hedge. Within a few metres of the tomb site is evidence of extensive ground disturbance and a collection of rusting farm machinery.

The landscape position of the monument is similar to others within the area. It has intervisibilty with the sea (Fishguard Bay), as well as the southern extent of the Mynydd Preseli. It is also not on the highest point within the immediate landscape—the land slopes upwards to the north. Visually, therefore, the monument would have commanded fertile undulating areas to the south and west. Approximately 1.7km to the south-west is the upland rock outcrop of Carn Llys and the siting of Ffyst Samson (also known as Trellysycoed). However, no intervisiblility exists between the two monuments. Ffyst Samson appears to be deliberately sited on the southern extent of the rock outcropping.

Despite its condition, Ffynnondruidion ('Druid's Spring') does have an interesting early archaeological past. In 1830, whilst levelling the site, labourers discovered two Neolithic flint artefacts; an axe (celt) and a stone adze. It is was believed axes were used for 'flaying victims, for which, in the opinion of a professional butcher to whom they were shown, they seemed admirably calculated'

Polished stone axe (Tenby A8) found at Ffynnondruidion

(Fenton's Tour, 1810, 24). The polished stone axe (Tenby A8) made from gabbro is now in Tenby Museum. The presence of these axes suggests two important activities. The first of these is an extensive trading network between axe areas, for the gabbro axe does not come from this area. According to Clough and Cummins (1988:139), the igneous stone used in its manufacture originates in Northern Ireland. The second concerns the use of these important, prestigious commodities in burial deposition. If intact, the site together with the finds, would have represented one of the richest Neolithic discoveries in this part of Wales.

Gyllwch/Garn Gilfach, Llanwnda

Sub-megalithic tomb cut into the rock
Location: Near the village of Trefasser, 4km west of Fishguard
(SM 9089 3898)
Access: By permission from the local farm

From the village of Mathry proceed north-west along the A487 towards Fishguard. Take the fourth turning left, signposted 'St Nicholas'. Drive through the village towards the hamlet of Trefasser. At a staggered crossroads just before the settlement, turn right onto a narrow winding country lane. Take the fourth turning on the left signposted 'Garn Gilfach', a 'No Through Road'. The burial chamber is sited on a small ridge, half way up Garn Gilfach, a large jagged rock outcrop. However, it is very difficult to locate — the capstone being only a few centimetres above present ground level and blending with the surrounding rock outcrops. Daniel (1950) suggests the chamber pit was cut and underpinned whilst the capstone lay *in situ*.

Garn Gilfach consists of a large, irregular low capstone (4.6m by 2.5m) supported by four uprights. It is argued that other possible uprights are in fact the collapsed remnants of drystone walling (Barker, 1992, 33). The tomb is sub-megalithic, in that the chamber is cut into the underlying bedrock. There is no evidence of a mound—the ridge appears to be too narrow. This type of sub-megalithic monument is similar in construction and landscape setting to others on the Strumble Head peninsula. To the outsider, including the archaeologist, these monuments remain inconspicuous within the surrounding landscape. However, whilst Garn Gilfach is certainly hidden within the landscape, it would have been known to those possessing the necessary ritual knowledge. An entrance into the main chamber appears to be located at the eastern end. Richard Fenton in 1811 (Fenton's Tour, 1811, 22-23) remarks that charcoal and pottery had been found at the site in 1800.

The views from this tomb recall those of nearby Ffyst Samson and Garn Wnda. All three possess commanding vistas of the dramatic rock outcrops on Strumble Head. Both Garn Gilfach and Ffyst Samson overlook the lowlands to the south and west, as well as St David's Head.

Garn Gilfach is also referred to as Gillfach Goch (Barnwell, 1872), Gilfach, Carn Gyllych (Grimes, 1936 & Daniel, 1950) and more recently, Garngilfach (Barker, 1992).

Garn Wen (3), Goodwick

Row of sub-megalithic rock cut tombs
Location: On the edge of Goodwick, near Fishguard (SM 948 390)
Access: On a public footpath

From Fishguard, drive to the ferry port of Goodwick on the A40. At a roundabout, just before reaching the town, take the second left into the village. A few metres along this road is a sharp turning to the left, but beyond the junction, take the first immediate right onto a narrow lane, signposted 'No Through Road'. Proceed up a steep incline for approximately 1.2km. At the end of the road is a small turning area and car park. To the right are open views across Fishguard Bay. On the left is a row of houses. Half way along the row is a narrow footpath which runs adjacent to the back gardens of the houses. The Garn Wen monuments, clearly visible, are sited directly behind the gardens and footpath in rough ground overgrown with bracken.

Above Goodwick is a line of at least three tombs that, when constructed and in use, would have commanded views right across Fishguard Bay and Dinas Head. Alas, these are now obscured by a row of houses. Nevertheless, the positioning of the tombs conforms to a pattern that is dominant throughout south-west Wales: that is, the tombs acknowledge only part of the landscape. Blocking views immediately behind the monuments is a large, deep-fissured rock outcrop (also known as Garn Wen).

The three tombs share a similar construction. Each is partly rock-cut (sub-megalithic) and was once incorporated within a round mound. The capstones, lying a few centimetres above the present ground level, are supported by low uprights. The southernmost tomb, known locally as Carrig Samson, is the best preserved of the three. It comprises five low uprights around a small polygonal chamber (Barker, 1992, 27). The capstone appears to be displaced.

In 1993, we visited the site and noticed a possible fourth tomb, of similar construction (with low supporting uprights) and in line with the other three, lying a few metres to the north. This also has an identical landscape outlook. As many as nine monuments were reported by the Pembrokeshire Archaeological Survey (Laws & Owen, 1897-1906). However, many slabs considered to be capstones in fact occur naturally.

Parc-y-Cromlech, Goodwick

Damaged chambered tomb
Location: On the edge of Goodwick, near Fishguard
(SM 9422 3907)
Access: By permission from Penrhiw Farm

From the Garn Wen monuments, proceed back towards the centre of Goodwick. Approximately 300m down the lane, take a sharp turning to the right to Penrhiw Farm, located about 600m from the turning. Parc-y-Cromlech stands in a large field to the right of the main farm buildings. Permission should be obtained from the farm before visiting this site.

Parc-y-Cromlech is very different from the nearby Garn Wen group. Also known as Penrhiw this, now badly-damaged tomb stands in a large south-facing field, and looks inland away from the sea to the north and east.

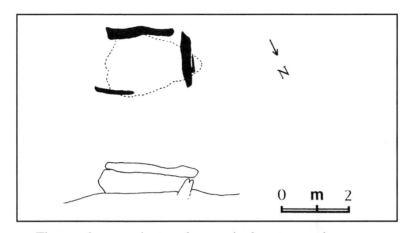

The tomb comprises a large, single, rectangular capstone supported by three uprights. The shape of the capstone and configuration of the three uprights suggest the chamber, too, was rectangular. Daniel (1950) remarks that the capstone had once been dislodged and was supported by only two uprights. The third upright has since been replaced. Littering the inside of the chamber, and around the outside edges of the three uprights, are numerous stones. These are either cairn material or the result of extensive field clearance. It was noted on a visit to Parc-y-Cromlech that several large stones abutting the monument appeared to be cut so as to form part of the tomb architecture, although this could be the result of frost shattering. There is no trace of any mound. However, if the chamber arrangement, in particular the uprights, are in their original position, a mound could be suggested to the west of the present monument, with the eastern extent of the chamber exposed to form a forecourt. Unfortunately, the ploughing regime within this field has been rather severe.

Carn Wnda, Llanwnda

'Earth fast' chambered tomb
Location: 3.5km east of Fishguard (SM 9331 3923)
Access: On a public footpath

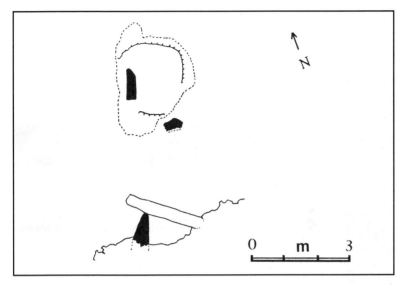

0   m   3

From Garn Gilfach chambered tomb, return to the narrow road and proceed south for 0.5km to a junction and turn left towards Penysgwarne. Follow the road for about 1.2 km and bear left for another kilometre. Turn left at the crossroads, with a cemetery on the left. Travel about 0.5km, bearing right and then left. The tomb is located 150m to the left of the road, half way up the rocky outcrop of Garnwnda.

Aligned north-west/south-east and sited on the north slope of Garnwnda, the capstone (4.6m by 2.8m) of this 'earth fast' chambered tomb rests on the edge of a rock-cut pit, and is supported at the north-west end by a single upright. As such, it is one of a number of 'sub-megalithic' tombs which make use of what Daniel calls a labour-saving 'makeshift device'. Developing the argument, Daniel follows Grimes in doubting that covering mounds were ever a significant component of these tombs. He says: 'They were probably originally surrounded by a low accumulation of stones sufficient to ensure that the chambers were efficient burial vaults and that they were not disturbed by beasts of prey' (Daniel, 1950, 48). The ledge on which the monument stands is anyway too small to have supported a covering mound. Constructed in this way, the Carn Wnda chambered tomb would have merged with the surrounding rock outcrop.

Although hidden from the valley below, this monument has outstanding views across Dinas Head

The plateau above that was probably used for ritual purposes when the monument was in use. This idea is based on the analysis of ritual monuments, in particular stone circles, stone rows and standing stones, which date from roughly the same period. These groups of monuments are always placed on flat areas of land. Recent research by the authors in Breconshire suggests that flat areas within rock outcrops were important spaces, which incorporated ritual activity (Children & Nash 2001).

An excavation inside the chamber revealed evidence of a cremation, indicating a possible Late Neolithic or Early Bronze Age date for the tomb. The burial consisted of a small urn made from a coarse and crumbly fabric and containing cremated bone (Fenton, 1848, 284).

The outlook of the monument takes in all the fertile lowland soils of Strumble Head. There is, however, no intervisibility with any other tomb. It appears to be the only tomb oriented in this way. All the rest point towards the south and west, and share a visual relationship with each other.

The St David's Group

The St David's Group (Landranger 157) comprises five monuments; Coetan Arthur, Carn Llidi, St Elvis Farm, White Horse and Treffynnon. All are locally orientated so as to incorporate a variety of landscape features. For example, three tombs are located within 0.5km of the sea. Two of these, Coetan Arthur and Carn Llidi overlook the sea itself, while St Elvis Farm deliberately ignores it. Both White Horse and Treffynnon are located in slightly undulating terrain and confront the jagged rock outcrops above St David's Head.

Coetan Arthur and Carn Llidi are 'earth fast' monuments and resemble those on Strumble Head. They are also located in similar rocky landscapes. Sited south of these tombs is Clegyr Boia, a Middle Neolithic settlement. The 'earth fast' tombs are probably a later architectural form, as they are less monumental than, for example, St Elvis Farm. However, the tombs and the Neolithic settlement are probably contemporary. One could imagine the settlers of Clegyr Boia placing the remains of their dead in either one of the two St David's Head monuments. The lack of architectural elaboration evident in these tombs should not detract from the idea that, towards the later Neolithic, the dead were considered special.

It is worth noting that further investigation of this now forbidding landscape is needed, especially as many 'earth fast' monuments may remain hidden. We would argue that the five monuments within this group, together with associated settlement and field systems, represent only a small fragment of a Neolithic landscape.

Coetan Arthur, St David's

> 'Earth fast' sub-megalithic tomb
> Location: 1.75km north of Whitesands Bay SM 7253 2805
> Access: Adjacent to the Pembrokeshire coastal path

Follow the Pembrokeshire coastal path north from the car park at Whitesands Bay towards St David's Head for about 1.75km. The capstone of Coetan Arthur is clearly visible from the path.

Not to be confused with the tomb of the same name near Newport, Coetan Arthur is located in a rocky coastal landscape overlooking the sea and the dramatic rock outcrops on St David's Head.

Grimes in 1936 argued that Coetan Arthur never had a prominent mound; and Daniel in 1950 believed that just enough stones were used to ensure 'efficient burial vaults'. He argues for a round barrow as the original tomb covering, and has cautiously identified a passage leading west from the chamber. The tomb was first excavated in 1898 by Baring Gould, who found virtually nothing except traces of a drystone lining, and, to the south-east, a small revetment wall.

Probably of Daniel's sub-megalithic 'earth fast' type, the chamber may have been formed by levering up one end of a stone lying *in situ* and supporting this with a 1.8m upright. Others have suggested the chamber represents a collapsed conventional form, as two further uprights have been identified lying beneath the capstone.

The capstone itself, which measures about 3.6m by 2.5m, resembles the outline of the nearby rocky ridge of Carn Llidi.

The landscape position of this monument, located around 50m above sea level, is unlike many others within the group. The nearest comparison would be the King's Quoit, at Manorbier. Located on a small peninsula jutting out into the Irish Sea, it is possibly associated with nearby settlement and field systems around Carn Llidi. It may also have links with the nearby Carn Llidi burial chambers located 1.3km to the east. However, the rocky landscape within which this monument stands slopes to the south-west and there is no intervisibility with the Carn Llidi burial chambers or the settlement and field systems.

When approached from the south, along the Pembrokeshire Coast Path, the monument can be clearly seen in silhouette from a distance of up to 2km, suggesting that the people who built it were concerned with visuality. There is no trace of a mound although there are large boulder-like stones around the monument. More importantly, the capstone does not merge into the landscape, as with other 'earth fast' monuments.

The idea that this site remained important to successive prehistoric communities is supported both by the existence of extensive Mesolithic scatters along the coastline to the north and south and Iron Age earthworks to the south.

Carn Llidi, St David's

Double-chambered tomb
Location: 0.5km north of Whitesands Bay (SM 7352 2789)
Access: Adjacent to the Pembrokeshire coastal path

Take the B4583 to Whitesands Bay. From the car park, take the
Pembrokeshire coastal path north towards St David's Head. The
chambered tomb lies about 0.5km from the car park. The outline of
the monument can be clearly seen from the footpath.

Sited on the rocky western slope of Carn Llidi, the tomb
comprises two chambers. The westerly chamber consists of an 'earth
fast' rock-cut pit with one end of the tilted capstone resting on the

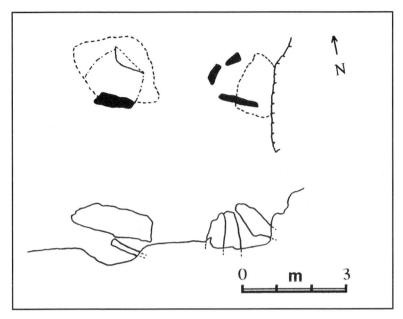

ground, while the other is supported by two upright stones. Daniel believes the easterly chamber once had its capstone placed horizontally, with one side resting on the ledge of the rock outcrop and supported on the other three sides by uprights inside a rock-cut pit.

There is no evidence of a covering mound at the site. Castleden (1992) believes that a mound once existed; but we consider it likely that mounds were not an important component of the rock-cut tombs in this area. Grimes argues that 'the mounds [of Carn Llidi and Carn Wnda] must have been small and could never have been elaborate' (Grimes, 1936, 12).

This tomb and nearby Coetan Arthur may have served the Neolithic settlement and field systems to the west. The monument has a similar landscape position to Carn Llidi, in that it is located on a western intermediate slope, which overlooks extensive prehistoric field systems. It is also placed within extensive rock outcropping and, like Carn Lidi, is inconspicuous within the surrounding landscape. It is likely that a settlement such as nearby Clegyr Boia existed close to the field systems.

St Elvis Farm, St Elvis

Double-chambered tomb
Location: 7km east of St Davids (SM 8120 2394)
Access: On a public footpath

About 1.75km east of Solva, itself east of St David's, turn right off
the A487, near a disused quarry. St Elvis Farm lies about 0.5km
from the main road along a public footpath. The tomb is also accessible from the Pembrokeshire coastal path, on the north coast of St
Bride's Bay.

Located on a north-west facing slope, the tomb is one of three
coastal burial sites in south-west Wales which appear to have been
purposely concealed from the sea.

The tomb seems to have been intact in 1890, when it was
described as a 'double cromlech'. Each capstone is supported by
two uprights, the largest measuring 3.7m by 3.1m. Today, both
structures are badly damaged; the photograph shows the western
chamber. It has been suggested that large stones found in nearby
walls may have been plundered from the monument. In 1798, a
tenant farmer from nearby St Elvis Farm was asked to stop
'blasting' bits of the tomb structure away (Fenton, 1810).

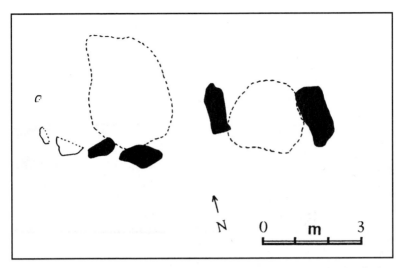

Although Daniel describes the tomb as 'morphologically inde-
terminate', the western chamber may be of his 'earth fast' type,
with the western end of the capstone resting on the ground and the
eastern end supported by uprights and forming the chamber
entrance. There are a few other examples of multiple chambers in
south-west Wales. One is the unusual five-chambered tomb of
Cerrig y Gof, others include The Hanging Stone, near Pembroke
and Carn Llidi on St David's Head.

Both chambers at St Elvis Farm are aligned north-west/south-
east, with capstones dipping towards an inlet of the River Solva.
They probably both had separate passages and entrances for there
does not appear to be any through passage linking the chambers.
Does this mean that the chambers were used by different family
groups? Many monuments, including St Elvis' Farm, possess enormous capstones. A large number of people would have been needed
to construct each monument and, more importantly, to manoeuvre
the capstone into place. This suggests corporate effort rather than
the involvement of single family groups.

White Horse, Llanhowell

Five uprights without a capstone
Location: 10km east-north-east of St David's (SM 8258 2839)
Access: By permission from Tresewig Farm

From the village of Croes-goch, on the A478 between St David's and Fishguard, turn onto the B4330 signposted 'Haverfordwest'. Take the first right down a narrow lane to the hamlet of Tresewig, by which name the tomb is also known. Opposite a farm, a track (and public footpath) leads due west. Follow the track for about 400m. The White Horse monument is located in the middle of a large field. Permission is required from Tresewig Farm before visiting this site.

The White Horse monument has never been excavated, as far as we are aware, but offers considerable research potential—much of the internal chamber appearing intact and undisturbed. In the recent past, the tomb has suffered extensive damage through field clearance. Indeed, both Rees (1981) and Barker (1992) noticed field clearance debris piled against the tomb. Furthermore, plough damage is noticeable up to the chamber itself (Barker, 1992).

White Horse has five chunky uprights, but no trace of a covering mound. In between the uprights, and in the chamber, the capstone has been 'placed' on edge. The chamber, probably rectangular, now contains soil and stone. This debris could possibly be contemporary with the monument's use. The size and original shape of the uprights and capstone would have been very similar to the Hanging Stone, near Pembroke. This would have made White Horse a very substantial and highly visible monument. There are also architectural affinities with Carreg Samson and Pentre Ifan; all three are truly megalithic. In spite of the damage inflicted by modern farming practices, White Horse is therefore a fine example of a portal dolmen type monument. Although there is no evidence of a mound, it appears that the surviving chamber forms part of a monument that was orientated north/south, based on a comparison of the chamber plan with those of Carreg Samson and Pentre Ifan. There may have been a doorway or entrance to the south (see photograph).

The surrounding landscape is very similar to that of the Treffynnon tomb. White Horse stands in gently undulating terrain with the peaks of St David's Head and local small rock outcrops clearly visible.

Treffynnon, Llandeloy

Damaged chambered tomb
Location: Near village of Treffynnon, east-north-east
of Fishguard (SM 8536 2866)
Access: By permission from farm in Treffynon

From the village of Croes-goch, on the A478 between St David's and Goodwick, take the B4330, following signs to Haverfordwest. Approximately 3km along this road take the third turn right sign-posted 'Treffynnon'. On reaching the hamlet, walk along a public footpath (directly opposite a farm) for 650m. The Treffynnon burial chamber stands on the edge of a large field (a bridleway runs adjacent to the south-east and the tomb may be approached by either path). Permission from the farm in Treffynnon is required before visiting this site.

The monument consists of a small single capstone which now rests on one of three uprights. The chamber is rectangular (2.2m by 1.5m), and is open on the northern side. This monument, like many others, has been used as a dump for field debris. Stones, possibly cairn material, litter both the chamber and the area around the

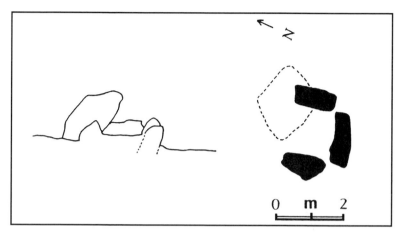

monument. There is no trace of any mound or cairn. Grimes (1939) suggests that Treffynnon is a simple chambered monument, one of three in the locality. However, its position within the landscape makes the monument highly visible. It may have possessed a small mound, possibly orientated north/south, with the chamber located at the northern end. The shape (plan) and present condition are similar to Penrhiw on Strumble Head.

Treffynnon stands on a slight south-facing ridge. The surrounding landscape is slightly undulating, but the tomb does

Side view of the Treffynnon monument, looking north-east

have views of the jagged peaks on St David's Head. Locally, a number of small rocky outcrops are also visible.

Although much smaller than its neighbour, White Horse, Treffynnon may be considered megalithic in form. Its capstone is similar to a number of 'earth fast' monuments within the Pembroke group, including the Devil's Quoit, King's Quoit and the Hanging Stone

The Inland Pembrokeshire Group

This group (Landranger 145 and 157) consists of nine monuments—Garn Turne, Parc-y-Llyn, The Altar at Colston, Carn Besi, Mountain, Gwal-y-Filiast and the Eithbed complex (north, central and south). Although listed as one group, this collection of monuments forms two main clusters. Garn Turne, Parc-y-Llyn and The Altar are all sited within an area of 2km². Both Parc-y-Llyn and The Altar are similar in size and shape. Their landscape setting is also comparable, but they are dwarfed by the massive capstone and forecourt of Garn Turne. None of these monuments is intervisible with another, but it is suggested that they were constructed and in use at

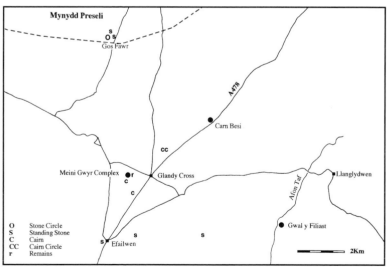

Spatial Distribution of Monuments around the South Preselis

89

the same time. Garn Turne may have 'acted' as the main nucleus or meeting place for local communities. Two of these communities, possibly small family units, were probably using Parc-y-Llyn and The Altar. Similar nucleated monuments with associated satellite tombs exist elsewhere within south-west Wales.

Farther north, and close to the southern extent of the Mynydd Preseli, is the Eithbed 'complex'. Here, three (or more) tombs are positioned in such a way that they face towards the south and St David's Head. Close by is Carn Besi, the Gors Fawr stone circle, the destroyed henge monument of Meini-Gwyr and a number of standing stones. All are located close to, but never on, the Mynydd Preseli. They may either be socially controlling the space around the south Preselis or, more importantly, establishing a boundary between familiar social space and the symbolic unknown of the mountains.

Like the Newport Group, this group of monuments offers a variety of architectural forms. In some cases, there may be a close association with certain Late Neolithic/Early Bronze Age monument groups, in particular those of Gors Fawr and Meini-Gwyr. These architectural differences probably represent change over time. Garn Turne, Mountain and Gwal-y-Filiast are probably early monuments, succeeded by those of Daniel's 'earth fast' classification. Others, such as Carn Besi and the Eithbed group, may need to be classified separately—we would describe them as simple slab monuments, probably dating from the Neolithic/Bronze Age transition.

Garn Turne, St Dogwells

> Long cairn with possibly the largest capstone in Britain
> Location: 11km south of Fishguard (SM 9793 2725)
> Access: There is public access to the site

From Fishguard, take the A40 towards Haverfordwest. At the village of Wolf's Castle, take the left turning towards Parc-y-Llyn. One kilometre along this lane, take the second left and proceed to a 'T' junction and St Dogwells Farm. Turn right along this lane for 1.5km. Garn Turne is located close to a large rock outcrop, about 40m from the lane.

Garn Turne (also known as Carn Turne and Garne Tarne), the largest of all the Inland Pembrokeshire Group, indeed the largest monument in south-west Wales, is one of three megaliths clustered around the hamlet of Colston. All three are approximately 10.5 km from the nearest coastline and with other monuments in the group appear to delineate the extent of the Mynydd Preseli.

The massive capstone (5m by 4.1m), one of the largest in Britain (weighing more than 60 tons), is now collapsed, resting on a series of dislodged uprights. An unusual 'V' shaped forecourt is similar to

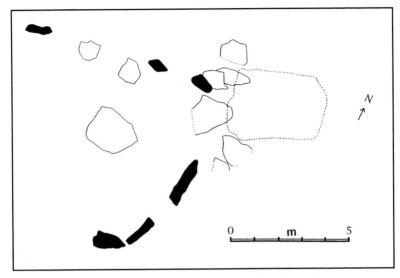

Plan of Garn Turne. Note the horned facade and massive capstone. This is very similar to the facade of Pentre Ifan

that of Pentre Ifan and the Irish Court Tombs of southern Ireland. Both Castleden (1992) and Houlder (1978) suggest the forecourt arrangement is 'familiar with the general western family of long cairns'. The forecourt and entrance to the chamber faces north-east towards a large rock outcrop. This may be replicated within the forecourt itself—a large, pointed sandstone conglomerate block is located within the central forecourt area. Outside the forecourt, and behind the now-damaged chamber, is a ridge outcropping which would have provided a solid foundation, as well as construction material, for the tomb itself.

Close to the rock outcrop and directly west of the monument is a boggy area that may have played a significant role in the ritual activity associated with the monument. It is interesting to note that when standing in front of the chamber and looking west, both sets of forecourt stones appear to visually embrace the rock outcrop and the area of bog.

Today, the tomb merges into its immediate surroundings—sited close to substantial localised rock outcropping. Indeed, so well is it 'hidden' within the landscape that, despite the monument's size, it

Looking south across Garn Turne

is difficult to locate. Apart from the nearby outcrop, the surrounding landscape is gently undulating. Nevertheless, the southern extent of the Mynydd Preseli is in full view. The question remains, how much of the stone construction of Garn Turne would have been visible: was this megalithic structure once entirely concealed beneath an earthen mound? Barker (1992, 29) does not entirely agree that this monument is a portal tomb. Rather, that it may be an 'earth fast' type. However, many of the 'earth fast' monuments within this region are located and constructed very differently. Furthermore, these monuments are small and unimposing. Others have suggested that the southern part of the monument, which incorporates the chamber and capstone, may have been part of a long cairn. However, the authors have found no evidence of this.

Apart from the monument and rock outcrop, there are several large monoliths that may form part of this impressive ritual landscape. Approximately 20m north-east of the monument is a single stone standing around 1.7m high. This is certainly prehistoric and may have served as a ritual marker between Garn Turne and another monument or a settlement. Other outlying monoliths exist close to the monument.

Parc-y-Llyn, Ambleston

Possible double-chambered tomb
Location: 12km south of Fishguard (SM 9823 2659)
Access: By permission from nearby farm

From the Garn Turne monument, head east along a narrow lane. About 1km along this lane is a crossroads. Turn right and then first right again. Parc-y-Llyn is sited in a small triangular field on the left, approximately 200m from the turning. Permission is required from the nearby farm to visit this monument.

Standing in the corner of a banked field, Parc-y-Llyn appears to be hidden away within a small secluded valley. Constructed of a small single capstone (2.5m by 1.8m) supported by four uprights, the monument has suffered much cattle damage in recent years. Many large stones, possibly belonging to a covering mound, are scattered nearby.

Within the field boundary to the east is a possible second chamber with one supporting upright. Other large stones, which may be uprights, are located north of the monument. According to Barker's plan (1992, 31), the entrance faces north-west, but appears not to be orientated to any particular nearby feature. However, 1km in the same direction is the Garn Turne monument. Very little of the regional landscape is visible. Similar landscape positioning is evident at The Altar, Colston, approximately 1.6km north of Parc-y-Llyn.

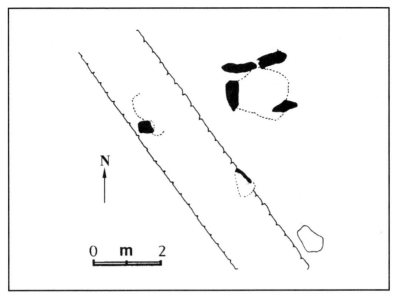

The monument stands on a small rise which slopes away towards a stream to the west. The chamber and the remains of the other possible chamber are aligned east/west. Barker (1992, 32) suggests both were enclosed within an elongated cairn, perhaps up to 15m in length. If this is the case, the entrance would be west-facing.

This double chambered monument has similar architectural traits to Cerrig Llwydion. Other chambers may have existed and the mound may have been considerably longer. It is also worth considering the state of preservation, in particular of *in situ* burial deposits within the possible second chamber beneath the field boundary. Also revealed may be any associated palaeo-soils.

The Altar, Colston, Little Newcastle

Small, damaged chambered tomb
Location: 10.5km south of Fishguard (SM 9828 2812)
Access: By permission from nearby farm at Colston

From the Parc-y-Llyn monument, proceed back to the crossroads and turn left. The Altar is located on a field boundary (next to the lane) on the right, approximately 2km from the crossroads. Permission is required from the nearby farm at Colston before visiting this monument.

The Altar at Colston, the third monument in this Inland Pembrokeshire Group, is also the smallest. Again, the tomb has suffered much cattle damage. However, half of the monument forms part of a hedge boundary and is therefore probably intact. When in use it would have been highly visible within the valley.

It consists of a small, rectangular, blocked capstone (2.2m by 1.9m) supported by at least three uprights. Barber and Williams (1989) have commented that a possible second megalith exists 40m due south of this monument. Apparently, a single pointed stone stands 1m above ground level, but is hidden within the boundary

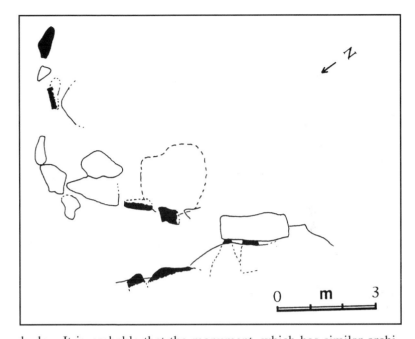

hedge. It is probable that the monument, which has similar architectural traits to the Devil's Quoit, King's Quoit and Hanging
Stone, comprised a single chamber and perhaps an associated
passage. Although The Altar is sited in a small valley, the southern
extent of the Mynydd Preseli is visible from the monument.
Nevertheless, we are convinced it shares a landscape affinity with
nearby Parc-y-Llyn, although the monuments differ architecturally
and therefore may have been in use at different times during the
Neolithic. However, what can be deduced is that this monument,
Parc-y-Llyn and Garn Turne were used for the interment of cremations. This being the case it is probable that the Altar and Parc-y-Llyn
and perhaps Garn Turne date from the late Neolithic, c.2500 BC.

Carn Besi, Llandyssilio East

Unimposing chambered tomb with impressive views
Location: 6.5km south-west of Crymach to the east of the
Mynydd Preseli (SN 1536 2768)
Access: Adjacent to the A478

The Carn Besi monument (also known as Dolwilim Dolmen) stands 6.5km south-west of the small village of Crymych alongside the A478. Located in a large open field, on the right when heading south, the tomb is clearly visible standing 10m from the road, opposite a small reservoir.

Carn Besi, easily the most unimpressive of all the monuments listed in this book, does, nevertheless, occupy a site with outstanding views over the northern and western extents of the Mynydd Preseli.

The monument consists of a small, single capstone supported by a number of short uprights no higher than present ground level. The capstone, orientated east/west, appears to point towards the general area of the Gors Fawr stone circle, 2.7km to the west. To the south, west and south-east there is much evidence of a Bronze Age landscape, which includes the stone circle, associated cairns and standing stones at Rosebush. Carn Besi possibly marks the northern boundary of this symbolic landscape. Despite the fact that it is undoubtedly Neolithic, the monument would have played an important role in organising and controlling later landscapes.

Its appearance suggests that Carn Besi, which, together with the examples at Eithbed, we have classified as single slab rather than 'earth fast' monuments, would have been known only to the people who used the monument: it merges so completely into the landscape.

Mountain, Mynachlog Ddu

Massive capstone on collapsed uprights, possibly a portal dolmen
Location: About 5km south-west of Crymych to the south-east of
the Mynydd Preseli (SN 1657 3286)
Access: Visible from a lane, or by permission from
Blaen Llethr Farm

From the village of Crymych, proceed south along the A478. Take
the first right-hand turning signposted 'Mynachlog-ddu'. Travel
along this narrow country lane for about 1km. At a T-junction, turn
left and drive for about 0.5km. The Mountain burial chamber, also
referred to as Llech y Gwyddon, is located in a marshy field opposite Blaen Llethr Farm, where permission to visit the monument
should be sought. The tomb is clearly visible from the road.

This is one of a series of monuments which encircle the Mynydd
Preseli. It would appear that this and other tombs within the group
mark the boundary between the unknown and 'dangerous' uplands
and the safety of the surrounding valleys.

The monument consists of a massive capstone (3.7m by 3.3m)
incorporated within a field boundary. When pristine, the Mountain

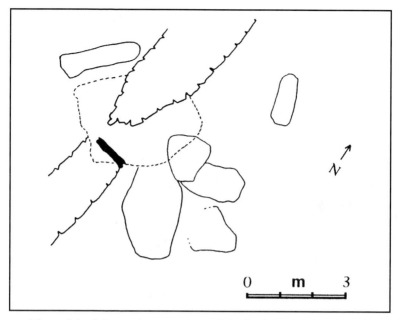

Plan of the Mountain monument. Much of the tomb has been incorporated within a boundary wall

monument would have been an impressive tomb, similar to that of The Hanging Stone in south Pembrokeshire. Lying prostrate around and beneath the capstone are five large stones, probably collapsed uprights. Other smaller stones are also present, including one that supports the capstone. Frances Lynch (1972, 81-82) remarks that Mountain is a portal dolmen which may have been centred within a round mound.

The fact that the monument has been incorporated into a large, earthen field boundary suggests that the foundations of the chamber, together with evidence of burial activity, may be intact. We have also noted what appears to be cairn debris within the field boundary. Originally, the chamber and orthostats would probably have been incorporated into an extensive mound orientated roughly north/south, with an entrance to the east, the mound being aligned with the present field boundary.

Gwal-y-Filiast, Llanboidy

> Impressive chambered tomb
> Location: About 6km south of Crymych to the east
> of the Preseli Mountains (SN 1705 2564)
> Access: On a public footpath

The Gwal-y-Filiast monument (also known as the Dolwilym Burial Chamber, Bwrdd Arthur and Gwalyfiliast) stands on a steep, wooded, west-facing ridge overlooking the Afon Taff. From Crymych, proceed south along the A478 to the hamlet of Glandy Cross. Turn left onto a road signposted 'Llanglydwen' which is reached after about 4km. Drive through the village, bearing right towards Login. About 0.75km along this road, turn right and park next to a wrought-iron farm gate on the right-hand side. The gate marks the start of a footpath which runs for 1km up to the Gwal-y-Filiast monument.

This impressive monument consists of a large single capstone supported by four uprights, which appear to delineate a polygonal chamber. A fifth upright was recorded by Barnwell in 1872, suggesting that this formed an entrance (facing east, down the slope).

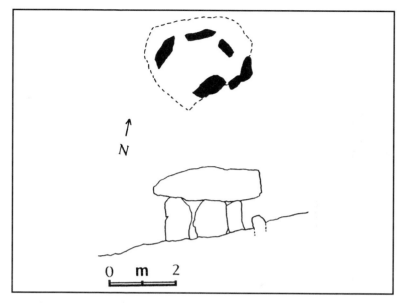

The capstone points towards the Afon Taff (to the west) and the eastern extent of the Mynydd Preseli. However, views of the mountains are obscured by thick woodland. At the point where the Afon Taff flows past Gwal-y-Filiast, the river becomes a violent rapid. This change in the river's character might have decided the tomb's location upon the ridge (Tilley, 1994). Other inland monuments in Wales follow a similar rule—Ty Isaf, Gwernvale, Garn Goch and Cwm Fforest, all within the Black Mountains Group and located close to running water.

Surrounding the monument is a series of kerbstones which possibly outline the remnants of an earthen mound. In 1872 it was claimed the mound/barrow still covered the chamber and capstone and that at least 32 outer kerbstones were also visible. This being the case, Gwal-y-Filiast must have suffered either large-scale vandalism or serious deterioration (or both) over the past 120 years. The shape of the kerbing suggests Gwal-y-Filiast once possessed a circular or, more probably, oval mound, making this one of only a handful of monuments in Wales (with this form of megalithic architecture) that have been incorporated into a mound of such shape.

Eithbed (North, Central, South), Maenclochog

> Badly damaged chambers of 'earth fast' tombs
> Location: South of the Mynydd Preseli (SN 080 286)
> Access: By permission from nearby farm

From the small village of Maenclochog, proceed north along the B4313, towards Rosebush. Just before entering the hamlet, take the first turn right signposted 'Glynaeron'. All three monuments are located along the southern edge of a field on the right-hand side, the second field from the turning. Permission to visit the tombs should be sought at the nearby farm.

The three Eithbed monuments (North, Central and South) are all, sadly, victims of recent field clearances and a scattering of large stones makes the actual identification of the monuments very difficult. The photograph above is of the largest and best-defined capstone. Stone clearances also took place between 1905 and 1909 (Barker, 1992, 52). Debate over whether two or three monuments exist at the site has continued for well over 120 years. Gardner Wilkinson (1871, 227) remarked that two (of the three) cromlechs were 'fallen'. Later, Done Bushell (1911, 300-1) recognised three capstones. Today, all are low-lying (almost at ground level), with little or no evidence of uprights or covering mound. They all may be similar in plan to the Carn Besi and Garn Wen monuments.

The largest tomb of the 'complex', The Goose Grave, was investigated by Done Bushell in 1911. Beneath the capstone, he found a pavement of flat slabs over traces of black ash. This black ash probably represents cremated human bone. If so, then this group of monuments sits squarely within the Late Neolithic/Early Bronze Age transitional period, when a trend towards cremation began to replace the practice of disarticulating human remains. Nineteenth- and early 20th-century antiquarian reports on other monuments in south-west Wales suggest similar findings, although there are those who feel that there is little evidence for burial. Tilley (1994: 109) has suggested that the acid soils have destroyed much of the burial evidence, except, that is, for cremated human bones which have been found, allegedly, in four monuments. In contradiction, Tilley also suggests that these monuments were neither used for burials nor deposition. However, it is clear from modern and antiquarian excavation that evidence for burial and deposition is quite significant (see Appendix C).

The monuments, plus the remains of burial chambers at Glandy Cross (Meini-Gwyr, SN 138 266), Carn Besi, Gwal-y-Ffiliast, and the burial chamber below Crug-yr-hwch (SN 167 329), appear to be deliberately placed around the southern hinterland of the Mynydd Preseli. All of them could either delineate and encompass a social/political territory, including the mountains, or mark a symbolic frontier between what is known, and what is unknown and dangerous (i.e. the Mynydd Preseli); no monuments appear to be sited within the mountains themselves.

The Eithbed group, together with Carn Besi, Mountain and possibly Parc-y-Llyn and the Altar, appear to be architecturally similar and were probably all in use at the same time.

The Meini-Gwyr Complex

Ritual monument complex
Location: Cilymaenllwyd (SN 142 267)
Access: Stone circle reached through a gate

From Carn Besi, proceed south along the A478 to the hamlet of Glandy Cross. Take the second right signposted 'Maenclochog'. The monument complex is located in fields south of this road, and is reached through a gate on the far side of the fourth house on the left.

Carn Besi, a cairn circle (SN 146 271), a series of standing stones (SN 137 255, SN 154 258 and SN 137 254) and the remains of a burial chamber (SN 145 255) may all be associated with this group of monuments. The largest monument within the complex is a henge comprising a stone-lined clay bank with a narrow, apparently stone-lined, entrance to the west. A pit in front of the entrance contained grey clay and fine charcoal fragments and probably had ritual significance. Within the henge, a circle of 17 stones (two of which are in the photograph above) measures 18.5m in diameter. An 18th-century drawing by William Stukely shows three large stone settings similar to the 'cove' at Stanton Drew, Somerset. Between the cove and the henge, to the west of the stone circle, were three pairs of stones. These monument groups may be compared with the large-stoned henge at Avebury, Wiltshire, the only missing component being a ditch. The monument possibly dates from the early 2nd millennium, i.e. the Late Neolithic (Grimes, 1938). Apart from the henge, there are the possible nearby remains of a burial chamber (SN 137 267) and a tumulus (possibly a barrow or cairn) (SN138 263).

The Pembroke Group

These eight monuments (Landranger 158)—the Devil's Quoit, The King's Quoit, Morfa Bycham A, B, C and D, The Hanging Stone and Twlc y Filiast—are constructed and located according to a number of different architectural and spatial patterns. However, a few of the tombs do seem to share some common rules, both in form and landscape setting. For example, The King's Quoit and The Devil's Quoit, although located in different landscapes, are similar architecturally. Both are 'earth fast', supported by a series of uprights at one end. Furthermore, the capstones of each monument are similarly shaped and are made from red sandstone. The four tombs on Ragwen Point—the Morfa Bycham Group—are all constructed, located and orientated in the same way. Although close to the sea, all seem to ignore it, their chambers and possible passage alignments pointing inland. This pattern is repeated in many of the coastal monuments of south-west Wales. The most obvious example is The King's Quoit at Manorbier. Here, the monument is just a few metres from the edge of the sea, but the capstone has been deliberately placed so as to point inland, towards the beach and headland. Others, like The Devil's Quoit and The Hanging Stone, are positioned in a more subtle way. Although close to the coast, they share no orientation, no relationship with the sea.

Three, perhaps four, architectural styles are used throughout this group, which may suggest either a localised building tradition, incorporating a symbolism unique to each monument, or, equally plausibly, different construction dates. Within the Neolithic core area of western Britain, new trends affected a monument's identity through time and space. Thus, small polygonal chamber-settings, supporting large boulder-like capstones were succeeded by tombs having flat, wedge-shaped capstones overlying square or rectangular chambers of the 'earth fast' type. Each monument is constructed so as to organise a social (public) and symbolic (private) space.

The idea of social, political and economic contact between Neolithic groups in south-west Wales and southern Ireland (Daniel 1950, Powell *et al* 1969) is interesting, even though the evidence is rather tenuous. A few artefacts from Northern Ireland, including several polished stone axes, have been found. In addition, there is, of course, the architecture of the monuments themselves. Within the Pembroke group, there appears to be no evidence of Irish architectural traits, with the possible exception of the Hanging Stone, a monument that bears some resemblance to the Irish Court Tombs in that, in plan, it forms a rectangular chamber which supports a massive capstone—a 'classic' portal dolmen type. However, the Hanging Stone (together with monuments such as Coetan Arthur and Llech-y-Tribedd) may equally be an indigenous affair. The architecture of Bedd-yr-Afanc (Newport group) represents the only other possible link to Ireland. By and large, however, the area appears not to have been influenced by the Irish Court Tombs and passage grave tradition. Rather, the Pembroke group (in complete contrast to the monuments of the Newport group or others south of the Preselis) comprises a series of small and unimposing tombs that appear to merge with the landscape. This is particularly true of the Morfa Bycham group, which, arguably, would have possessed no covering mound. Our view is that these monuments served small farming communities that exploited both land and sea. For these communities, the idea of strictly defined territories may have been less important than it was in other areas.

Devil's Quoit, Angle

'Earth fast' tomb
Location: 10km west of Pembroke (SM 8865 0084)
Access: Clearly visible from road

The Devil's Quoit (also known as Broomhill Burrows) is located in a large, open field close to the B4320. From Pembroke, proceed west along the B4320 for approximately 10km, towards the coastal village of Angle. The Devil's Quoit is clearly visible standing on a small rise in a field 100m from the road and just before a left turn (signposted 'Castlemartin').

The monument consists of a capstone supported at the western end by three uprights. At the opposite end, the capstone is set firmly into the earth. Daniel (1950) refers to this construction as 'earth

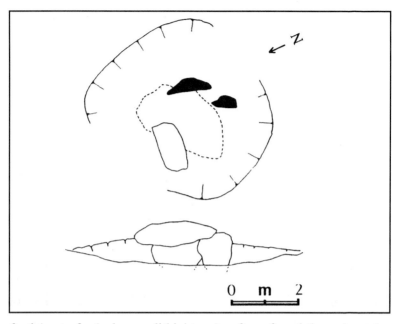

fast' (part of a 'sub-megalithic' type), a form found throughout the region. Barker (1992, 38) suggests that, in this particular case, the term 'earth fast' is misleading because the capstone sits on an earthen surface that may not be contemporary with the construction of the tomb. The capstone, made from local sandstone, is similar in shape to the King's Quoit at Manorbier. There appears to be no trace of a mound, but the chamber is set within a shallow depression (Barker, 1992)

Although located on a small ridge, the tomb does not look out towards the open sea but rather takes in a visual sweep of Milford Haven Sound, 5km to the north. Other tombs which similarly ignore the sea are Trellyffant, Llech-y-Tribedd and nearby St Elvis Farm. Approximately 150m to the east of the Devil's Quoit is an extensive sand dune system, possibly representing an ancient sea inlet (known as Kilpaison Burrows). The soils immediately surrounding the Devil's Quoit are predominantly sandy in texture, the field possibly being part of the dune system.

King's Quoit, Manorbier

'Earth fast' chambered tomb
Location: Manorbier Bay (SM 0593 9728)
Access: Adjacent to the Pembrokeshire coastal path

From the historic coastal village of Manorbier, walk south along the Pembrokeshire coastal path. The King's Quoit can be clearly seen, approximately 300m from the beach at Manorbier Bay.

The King's Quoit has one of the most dramatic landscape settings in south-west Wales. It is one of only a few monuments located in sight of the open sea. Others include Carreg Samson, Garn Wnda, Coetan Arthur, Carn Llidi and the four rock-cut monuments of Morfa Bycham A, B, C, and D.

The monument itself is located on a small bank above a cliff face and comprises a huge single capstone supported by two uprights—although there is a third upright located at the south-eastern end, which is now probably collapsed. The position of the three uprights suggests the chamber was originally rectangular.

The monument may be regarded as 'earth fast', belonging to the sub-megalithic classification (Daniel, 1950). The capstone, made

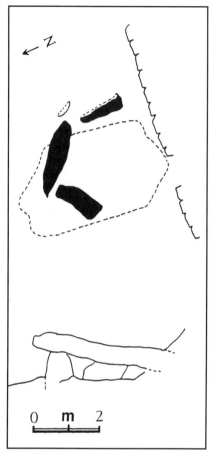

from local sandstone, points inland towards Manorbier Bay. This suggests that the King's Quoit is to some extent ignoring the sea. Its builders and users are quite clearly orientating the monument inland.

The King's Quoit was once regarded as a natural 'accidental formation' of stone (Anon, 1851, 315). Recently, Barker (1992, 38) has supported Daniel's 'earth fast' classification. We believe no covering mound would have existed during the Neolithic because the ledge on which the monument stands is far too narrow. This being so, The King's Quoit is similar in construction to, and shares a comparable landscape setting with, both Garn Gilfach and nearby Devil's Quoit.

Its position within the landscape is quite interesting. The King's Quoit is by far the largest 'earth fast' monument in south-west Wales and, if it is assumed that it had no covering mound, it would have been visible, on land or sea, from some way off. Located on a north-facing ridge above Manorbier Bay, the King's Quoit has commanding views of the surrounding landscape and would have been an important marker for those using the bay and headlands to the north and south.

Morfa Bycham A, B, C, & D, Marros

Four (or five) chambered tombs (A and B shown above)
Location: Near Pendine, south-west of St Clears (SM 22 07)
Access: Adjacent to the Pembrokeshire coastal path

Ignore the recent Ordnance Survey 'Pathfinder' map for this area. The map clearly shows the tombs to be located about 100-200m west of their actual position (inland, behind Ragwen Point).

From the village of Pendine, follow the coastal path westwards for approximately 1.8km. The path is, in places, very steep and rugged, so extreme care should be taken. The path winds past Gilman Point, across a small pebbled beach and up a steep rocky incline. All four monuments are sited among rock debris and merge into the surrounding landscape.

Interestingly, the monuments would have been difficult to locate during their use. We would argue that the siting of this cemetery would be a deliberate act. During the Neolithic, only those with special ritual knowledge may have known the precise whereabouts of each monument. Similar monument locations are evident within the coastal headlands of this part of Wales (see above).

The landscape seen from these monuments is extremely dramatic. All four tombs are aligned north/south, and all appear to face Gilman Point rather than the sea (like the capstone of the King's Quoit, Manorbier). Pendine Sands and the surrounding headland are clearly visible beyond Gilman Point. In addition to the four monuments mentioned below, a possible long chambered mound is located to the west, above the extensive rock outcropping between Morfa Bycham B and C. Barker quite rightly refers to this series of monuments as the Morfa Bycham cemetery (1992, 10). Morfa Bycham A, B and C are intervisible with each other and all are similar in construction. Morfa Bycham D, a submerged monument, set within the loose rock debris, is closest to the outcropping.

Morfa Bycham A (SM 2213 0743)

Morfa Bycham A, one of the four tombs located on Ragwen Point, is the farthest south of the group. It comprises a single capstone, now dislodged from its original position. It was originally supported by nine uprights. The stone material is local, possibly frost-shattered debris from the nearby cliff face. The chamber is rectangular (2m by 1.5m), with evidence of a passage (Castleden, 1992). This, plus remnants of an oval cairn, place Morfa Bycham A in the passage-grave tradition. Its landscape setting suggests the tomb could be compared with the Anglesey passage grave of Barclodiad-y-Gawres.

114

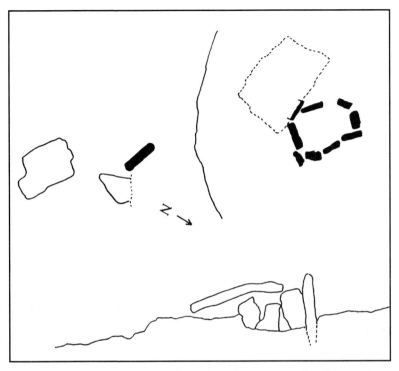

Castleden (1992) suggests the other three may also be passage graves. If this is the case, then the Morfa Bycham monuments are the only possible examples in this part of Wales.

When visiting this monument in 1993, we saw little or no evidence of either a passage or cairn material. The whole area in front of the cliff face was littered with weather-shattered rock debris. We suggest the tomb's morphology represents very much a localised tradition, utilising local materials, the uprights and capstones being shaped by nature, rather than by design. In the case of Morfa Bycham D, there is evidence of a single passage upright, but this is by no means conclusive evidence that it is a passage grave.

This monument, along with Morfa Bycham B, C and D, was excavated and restored during the early part of this century (1910-11). A few artefacts were found within a stratified sequence within the chamber, the southern part of which contained a small collection of lithics, including scrapers and waste flake material. Also found were charcoal and a few fragments of bone (Ward, 1918). The artefacts, according to Ward (1918, 69-70), overlay a 'rude pavement'.

Morfa Bycham B (SM 2214 0748)

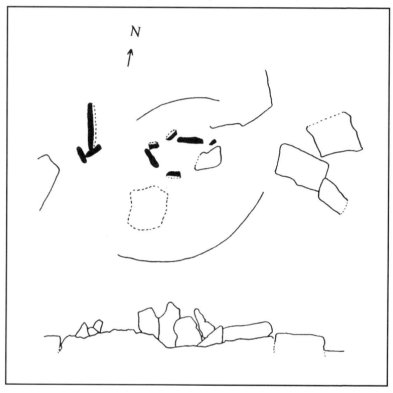

Morfa Bycham B stands on a natural ledge about 50m north of Morfa Bycham A. Here, there is evidence for a small cairn on the southern extent, but certainly no passage. Barker (1992, 12) questions whether or not this monument had a proper entrance. However, the authors suggest that a possible entrance may be located to the south, facing the open sea. A similar 'opening' exists at Morfa Bycham A. According to Gardner Wilkinson (1870, 42-3), the cairn, pear-shaped, was surrounded by kerbing. However, rock debris now covers any traces. In the vicinity of the cairn are two large flat slabs—one, a possible displaced capstone. The chamber, now much disturbed, is pentagonal and consists of six or seven (confused) uprights which open out to the north-west. It was excavated on a single day, May 17, 1910, by Treherne, Gibbins, Clarke and Ward. Apart from discovering previous excavation disturbance, three flint flakes were found (Ward 1918).

Morfa Bycham C (SM 2216 0754)

Approximately 70m south of Morfa Bycham B is the third tomb. According to Castleden (1992), this tomb, now much damaged, consists merely of a 'collection' of stones. We noted a small section of what may be a capstone, and at least ten uprights—arranged as a polygonal chamber and passage—as well as traces of a low mound. Barker (1992) mentions that the chamber area is 'Y' shaped. The six uprights leading from the chamber and forming the passage are approximately 2.5m long. The plan may actually reveal a possible double-chambered monument. The two chambers appear to be aligned east/west and separated by their own uprights. There is no trace of any entrance to either structure.

This monument is intervisible with Morfa Bycham A and B, but not with D. Morfa Bycham A, B and C have definite landscape affinities which are seaward. However, Morfa Bycham D, although intervisible with the sea, is orientated inland. The three seaward monuments are constructed in a similar fashion.

Morfa Bycham D (SM 2216 0762)

The fourth monument within this group is possibly the most interesting. Again, located on a natural ledge, just below the cliff face,

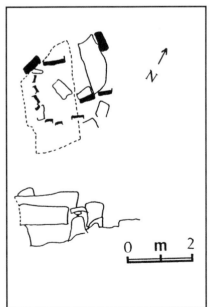

Morfa Bycham D has a chamber submerged within the rocky soil.

The large capstone (almost at ground level) covers a rectangular chamber and is supported by at least 11 uprights, with irregular drystone walling between. Outside, there is a possible small, low earthen mound. Cut into the mound, and—unusually—at the side of the chamber, is an entrance with a doubtful passage. Two uprights are positioned on the north-western cut. Immediately to the west of this cut is a large slab, which may be a passage roofing stone. The entrance looks out towards Gilman Point and Pendine Sands beyond.

The tomb was discovered by Treherne and Evans on June 11, 1910 and excavated a few days later. The massive capstone (4.1m by 2.3m) and passage were partially covered by loose cairn rubble. The chamber entrance was blocked by a small slab. Inside the chamber was 'a considerable accumulation of brownish soil, on the surface of which lay bones of recent animals' (Ward, 1918, 72-3). The excavation was halted when it was discovered that the capstone had become unsafe. The excavators found the original chamber floor but no artefacts.

Morfa Bycham Long Barrow

Although we have not included the monument within the inventory, there is some evidence of a Neolithic long barrow on headland above the rocky outcrops on which the Morfa Bycham monuments stand. The monument has been described as a wedge-shaped long cairn aligned north-east to south-west and measuring 20m x 10m (Murphy, 1985). Standing at a maximum height of 1.5m, this monument was first recorded by Treherne in 1926. Treherne states that, on the western side—what he refers to as The Altar—was a large collection of cairn material. However, Barker questions (1992:43) whether the monument is in fact prehistoric at all. If this is indeed a long chambered tomb, then it is probably earlier than the four Morfa Bycham monuments. This is because the long barrow tradition significantly pre-dates the 'earth fast' and subterranean monuments within south-west Wales, which appear to be a Late Neolithic/Early Bronze Age type.

The Hanging Stone, Burton

Double dolmen or possible passage grave
Location: Near Hill Mountain, 5km north of Pembroke
(SM 9722 0822)
Access: On a public footpath

The Hanging Stone forms part of a field boundary and is located just south of the village of Hill Mountain on a public footpath. From the village (5km north of Pembroke), proceed north-west to the hamlet of Sardis. Take the first turn left to Burton. Approximately 400m down this lane is a footpath on the left. Follow the footpath for 250m and the Hanging Stone lies just beyond the convergence of two field boundaries.

The surrounding landscape is gently undulating. Milford Haven Sound, approximately 3km to the south, is clearly visible from the top of the capstone. The monument is described by Grimes (1939), and later by Daniel (1950), as a possible passage grave. Today, the tomb consists of a very large and substantial capstone (3.1m by 2.6m) supported by three uprights. The chamber appears to be polygonal and, until 1864, it was reported that drystone walling was

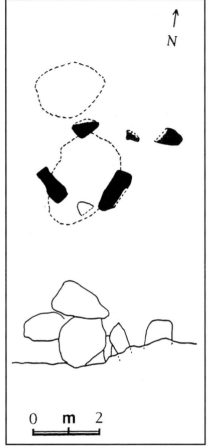

N

0   m   2

visible in between the uprights. Also present was a substantial amount of possible cairn material. Alas, this, plus any evidence of a covering mound, has long since gone. However, in a nearby hedge there is a possible second capstone and two uprights (seen on the left of the photograph). Both Grimes (1939) and Lynch (1975) suggest that these stones may represent 'the vestiges of a short passage'. We are of the opinion that the Hanging Stone and the nearby displaced second capstone and dislodged uprights are in fact two chambers forming a double dolmen. Other examples of multi-chambered tombs exist elsewhere in south-west Wales, for example, St Elvis Farm, Trellyfant and Twlc y Filiast.

It should also be noted that, if the capstone is incorporated into the hedge boundary, then there may be further remains, including a chamber, orthostats and, perhaps, burial remains, beneath. The survival of human remains, or any other environmental deposition, would be enhanced by the fact that this monument lies within a non-acidic soil area, the limestone and sandstone rich soils assisting the preservation of bone.

Twlc y Filiast, Llangynog

Chambered tomb
Location: About 8km south-west of Carmarthen (SN 3383 1608)
Access: On scrubland adjacent to a public footpath

From the historic town of Llanstephan (Landranger 159), proceed north towards Llanybri. From the centre of the village, follow the road to Llangynog (approximately 3km). From the local village school, follow a recently-laid public footpath to a small stream. On the right-hand side is a rusted metal fence. Cross the fence and continue parallel to the stream. The Twlc y Filiast monument is clearly visible on rough scrubland approximately 20m from the fence.

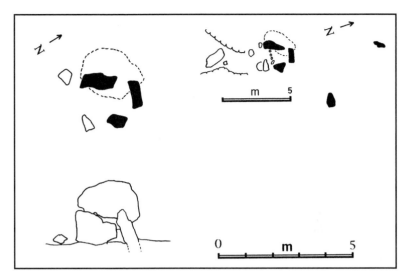

Plan of Twlc y Filiast. The main drawing is after Barker, the top right is adapted by the authors

Twlc y Filiast (also known as 'Ebenezer' and Arthur's Table) is one of a handful of megalithic monuments in total isolation from the main megalith clusters within south-west Wales. Its landscape setting is very similar to that of many tombs in the South Wales hinterlands. The monument lacks intervisibility with the sea, despite standing only 5.5km from the coast. The tomb should, therefore, be classified as an inland monument. Both Daniel (1950) and Houlder (1978) remark that Twlc y Filiast is hidden, lying in a steep-sided valley with a small stream running by.

The tomb comprises a small rectangular chamber of three uprights. A displaced capstone located outside the chamber is supported by two of the uprights. Houlder (1978) argues that the chamber is in fact trapezoidal. Earlier investigations found no trace of a covering mound (Daniel, 1950). However, an excavation carried out in 1953 by Hubert Savory discovered the remnants of an elongated mound (18m by 9m), a possible ante-chamber and a series of ritual pits. The mound is orientated north-north-east/south-south-west, following the axis of the valley. One side of the mound has been eroded by a small brook. On a recent visit to this site, it was noted that seven or so stones appeared to delineate a possible narrow passage and facade. These additions could establish Twlc y Filiast as an important site, especially as it is located away from the main Pembroke Group.

The 1953 excavation yielded very few artefacts. Nothing at all was found in the chamber. However, a small flint scraper, a stone pendant and a few fragments of unidentifiable pottery were recovered close by, the flint scraper and stone pendant being retrieved from cairn material immediately outside the chamber area. The pendant—or amulet (as described by Lynch 1969:167)—may represent a metal axe. If so, then the monument was clearly in use during the Late Neolithic/Early Bronze Age (*c*.2000-2500 BC). Savory considered that Twlc y Filiast had been extensively damaged, especially within the entrance area, but the plan of the monument suggests that it is architecturally related to the Portal Dolmen tradition.

Isolated Monuments — Carmarthenshire

Most of the monuments discussed have fitted comfortably within a series of clusters. However, there will always be one or two that refuse to conform. The Cerrig Llwydion (double) dolmen may be designated as an isolated monument to the extent that its nearest definite neighbour is well over 20km away to the south (Twlc y Filiast), although Barker (1992) recognises a possible chambered monument 8km to the north-east — Yr Hen Llech. Our analysis reveals that the mean distance between tombs in this part of Wales is between 2 and 3km. It is most probable, therefore, that Cerrig Llwydion, and for that matter, Bedd Taliesin, some 70km north, near Aberystwyth, would, at one time, have been part of a more concentrated distribution.

Cerrig Llwydion is a substantial tomb incorporating two chambers with a possible long mound, perhaps having similar dimensions to that of Pentre Ifan, near Newport. If this is the case, then other smaller tombs may have been located close by. The presence of Bronze Age barrows and cairns in the vicinity indicates ritual and symbolic continuity within the landscape. It could be suggested that the Cerrig Llwydion dolmen housed at least two members of a ranked society, with one burial per chamber. The erection of single burial barrows and cairns during the subsequent Bronze Age would have carried on the 'tradition' of high-status single burials. On this basis we suggest the monument was constructed and in use during the Late Neolithic, and was possibly contemporary with the smaller 'earth fast' tombs farther south.

Cerrig Llwydion, Cynwyl Elved

> Chambered tomb
> Location: About 10km north of Carmarthen (SN 3738 3258)
> Access: By permission from nearby farm

From the small market town of Newcastle Emlyn (Landranger 145), proceed south for 15km along the A484 towards Carmarthen. Just before the village of Cwmduad, take a sharp turning right onto a farm track to Nant-clawdd uchaf Farm (100m). From the farm, walk west along a field boundary for 200m. Cerrig Llwydion is located a few metres north of the point where another field intersects the western boundary. It is clearly visible from this point. Permission is required from the farm before visiting the site.

Cerrig Llwydion is one of a handful of monuments benefiting from the protection afforded by being incorporated into a boundary wall. Little evidence of a covering mound exists. However, disturbance in the field to the east of the monument could represent mound material. Large stone blocks—possible cairn remains or even part of the tomb chamber—are visible.

The large, irregular elongated capstone of the monument is supported at the northern end by three uprights over a small rectan-

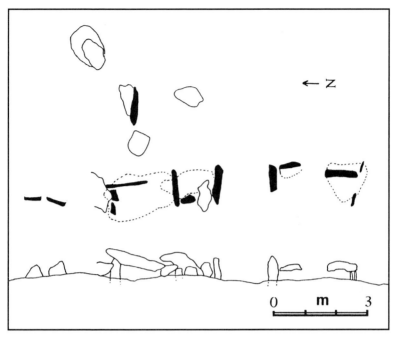

gular chamber. The capstone (and therefore the chamber) is, unusually, orientated north/south. Directly behind the main capstone is a smaller slab and what appears to be an extension of the main chamber. Approximately 3m behind the main chamber is a second chambered structure comprising a capstone and five uprights (Barker, 1992). Daniel (1950) classifies this monument as a large cist. We firmly believe that Cerrig Llwydion is a double dolmen of massive proportions. It is suggested that the mound, possibly oval or rectangular in shape, measures well over 21.3m by 15.5m

Although isolated from other similar monuments, Cerrig Llwydion lies within a dense concentration of Bronze Age barrows. The landscape is bare, almost moor-like, the barrows dominating all of the high ground. However, the tomb is typical of megalithic monuments in Wales in that it is positioned on a ridge, rather than upon the highest point in the landscape. It overlooks a river valley, dominant views of which are had to the south and east.

Appendix A The Chambered Monuments of South-West Wales

Name	Parish	Grid Ref	Metres O.D.	Coastal/ Inland	Km from coast
Newport Group					
Bedd-yr-Afanc	Meline	1087 3457	142	I	0.8
Pentre Ifan	Nevern	0994 3701	145	C	4.2
Cerrig y Gof	Newport	0365 3890	46	C	0.8
Carreg Coetan	Newport	0602 3935	8	C	0.5
Trellyffant	Nevern	0822 4252	137	I	0.5
Llech-y-Tribedd	Moylgrove	1005 4319	188	I	0.6
Fishguard Group					
Carreg Samson	Mathry	8483 3350	42	C	0.3
Trewalter Llwyd	Mathry	8682 3176	98	C	2.0
Ffyst Samson	St Nicholas	9059 3492	128	C	2.3
Ffynnondruidion	St Nicholas	9204 3679	107	I	3.4
Gyllwch/Garn Gilfach	Llanwnda	9089 3898	183	C	1.9
Garn Wen (3)	Goodwick	948 390	122	C	0.3
Parc-y-Cromlech	Goodwick	9422 3907	100	C	1.0
Carn Wnda	Llanwnda	9331 3923	173	C	1.0
St David's Group					
Coetan Arthur	St David's	7253 2805	38	C	0.3
Carn Llidi	St David's	7352 2789	122	C	0.9
St Elvis Farm	St Elvis	8120 2394	61	I	0.4
White Horse	Llanhowell	8258 2839	91	I	4.1
Treffynnon	Llandeloy	8536 2866	125	I	4.4
Preseli Group					
Garn Tune	St Dogwells	9793 2725	137	I	10.2
Parc-y-Llyn	Ambleston	9823 2659	128	I	11.1
The Altar, Colston	Lt Newcastle	9828 2812	115	I	10.1
Carn Besi	Llanissilio East	1536 2768	236	I	-
Mountain	Mynachlog Ddu	1657 3286		I	-
Gwal-y-Ffiliast	Llanboidy	1705 2564	245	I	-
Eithbed (North)	Maenclochog	0796 2860	243	I	-
Eithbed (Central)	Maenclochog	0796 2860	243	I	-
Eithbed (South)	Maenclochog	0796 2860	243	I	-
Pembroke Group					
Devil's Quoit	Angle	8865 0084	37	C	0.7
King's Quoit	Manorbier	0593 9728	18	C	0.1
Morfa Bycham A	Marros	2213 0743	75	C	0.2
Morfa Bycham B	Marros	2214 0748	100	C	0.2
Morfa Bycham C	Marros	2216 0754	11	C	0.2
Morfa Bycham D	Marros	2216 0762	120	C	0.2
The Hanging Stone	Burton	9722 0822	75	I	8.6
Twlc y Filiast	Llangynog	3383 1608	100	I	5.5
Isolated Monument					
Cerrig Llwydion	Cynwyl Elved	3738 3258	250	I	-

Appendix B
(i) Damaged and Doubtful Monuments
   (after Barker 1992, Daniel 1950 & Grimes 1936)
(ii) Lost Monuments

(i)

Name	Parish	Grid Ref	Allied Group	Generic Type	Visible Evidence
Carn Menyn	Mynachlog Ddu	1404 3262	Newport	Round cairn?	Capstone & 3 uprights
Cefn Brafle	Llanboidy	1957 2294	Preseli	Chambered	Capstone & 2 uprights
Cuckoo Stones	Carew	0646 0387	Pembroke	Chambered	Capstone & uprights
Fron Ucha	Llanstephan	3454 1074	Pembroke	Chambered	2 uprights
Llan	Lampeter Velfrey	147 140	Pembroke	2 chambers?	4 & 3 uprights
Llecha	Llanhowell	8115 2710	St David's	Burial chamber?	Recumbent stones
Lower Treginnis	St David's	7180 2360	St David's	Small cairn?	2 uprights? & 2 blocks
Morfa Bycham	Marros	2213 0751	Pembroke	Long cairn?	Elongated mound
Quarry Bach	St Lawrence	9300 2687	Preseli	Cist	Capstone & 1 upright
Yr Hen Llech	Llangeler	4128 3602	(Isolated)	Large cist	Capstone & 1 upright

(ii)

Name	Parish	Grid Ref	Allied Group	Generic Type	Visible Evidence
Coatan Arthur	Llanllawer	683 617	Fishguard	Cromlech	No visible remains
Croeswdig	St David's	26 73	St David's	Cromlech	No visible remains
Cuffern Cromlech	Roch	8995 2225	St David's	Cromlech	No visible remains
Glynmael	Fishguard	966 369	Fishguard	Cromlech	No visible remains
Kingheriot	Whitchurch	810 261	Pembroke	Cromlech	No visible remains
Llandruidion	St David's	7865 2494	St David's	Circular mound	No visible remains
Llanunwas	Whitchurch	787 242	Pembroke	Cromlech	No visible remains
Llech yr Ast	Llangeler	40 35	Preseli	Ruined cromlech	No visible remains
Man y Gromlech	Llanwnda	909 389	Fishguard	?	No visible remains
Parc y Goetan	St David's	7713 2920	St David's	Cromlech	No visible remains
Phos y Gilwen	St David's	7730 2927	St David's	Cromlech	No visible remains
Prysg	Maenclochog	0956 2711	Prerseli	Cromlech	1 by 2m stone?
Stone Park	Rubaxton	9624 1971	Pembroke	Ruined cromlech	No visible remains
Trefach	Nevern	0639 3505	Newport	Ruined cromlech	No visible remains
Trefael	Nevern	1030 4030	Newport	Burial chamber	Cupmarked stone
Waun y felin	Llanstephan	3504 1126	Pembroke	Small cromlech	Capstone & 3 uprights
Y Garn	Llanwnda	9142 3911	Fishguard	cromlech?	No visible remains

Appendix C   Excavators and Excavations

Site	Date of Excavation	Excavator	Significant finds
Bedd-yr-Afanc	1939	Grimes	
Pentre Ifan	1936-37, 1958-59	Grimes	charcoal, flint, pottery
Cerrig y Gof	1810	Fenton	bone, charcoal, pottery, stone objects
Carreg Coetan	1979-80	Rees	bone, charcoal, pottery
Carreg Samson	1968	Lynch	bone, pottery
Ffynnondruidion	1810	Fenton	stone
Gyllwch/Garn Gilfach	1810	Fenton	charcoal, flint, pottery
Carn Wnda	1848	Fenton	bone, pottery
Coetan Arthur	1899	Baring Gould	
St Elvis Farm		Oswald	
Morfa Bycham A	1910	Treherne, Giddins, Clarke, Ward	bone, charcoal, flint
Morfa Bycham B	1910	Treherne, Giddins, Clarke, Ward	flint
Morfa Bycham D	1910	Treherne, Giddens, Clarke, Ward	
Twlc y Filiast	1953, 1956	Savory	charcoal, bone, flint, pottery, stone objects

Appendix D   Statementing the Axe

The polished stone and flint axe may be considered one of the most important components of burial deposition in Neolithic Britain. Concerning the social and symbolic aspects of the axe, Mark Edmonds in his seminal work *Stone Tools and Society* (1995) suggests that it represents much more than an everyday tool. Likewise, Tilley (1993) suggests axes were an extremely important part of the ritual of burying the dead.

There appear to be a number of complex issues surrounding the deposition of axes within burial monuments. It is obvious that they were an item of beauty and prestige—neither polished flint nor stone axes could have been used to perform any kind of mundane task. However, twice as many axes have been found outside monuments as have been found within burials. This suggests that the living also used axes and that they were not just an item that accompanied the dead on their journey to the next world. It is more than probable that they had an important social function—that they were used for trading and exchange. It is interesting that, in south-west Wales, there is evidence of both exchange/trading (from stray finds) and burial deposition. More importantly, many axes appear to be coming in from other areas, suggesting that power and prestige was to be gained by acquiring axes from production centres outside the locality.

Located within the Mynydd Preseli, is a major source for the production of axes. This source forms part of a national group of axe mines and quarries which are summarised by Houlder (1988). This report lists a total of 89 polished stone and flint axes found within Pembrokeshire and a further 41 and 45 in Cardiganshire and Carmarthenshire respectively. Approximately 40 per cent of these are from specific axe-manufacturing areas, the majority of which lie within the Preselis. In addition, there may be axes which are held in private collections or discovered since 1988. The authors believe the actual total is very much higher. Certainly, the number of green-stone axes, in particular from Cornwall, is higher than the single specimen published within the Clough & Cummins report (1988). A few axes from North Wales have also been found.

It is clear that, since the early Neolithic, both indigenous and expeditionary groups have used stone from the Preselis as a prestige raw material. Three individual quarries have been recognised, forming part of a national petrological group which is numbered 1-24 (I-XXIV). Darvill (1987, 55) and others have recognised one of these as an early stone source (Group VIII [igneous tuff] - 3,000-2,500 BC) located around the southern extent of the Mynydd Preseli. The other two groups, XIII and XXIII, [spotted dolerites] are of a later date—after 2,500BC. Pitts (1980, 8) has suggested that igneous tuff has a predominant flaking characteristic, while dolerites are best worked using a pecking technique. Both techniques would have been ideal for shaping rough-outs from the source areas. Both types of stone would have served different uses: the tuffs for axes and the dolerites for perforated implements (plates pp. 15 & 71). Within the area, both types are well represented. Outside south-west Wales, in particular within the fertile Cotswold-Severn region, axes from the Preselis occur frequently, while Savory (1980, 223) suggests dolerites from Groups XIII and XXIII also occur in North and South Wales, but infrequently. This pattern suggests the coastal communities were considered to be valuable trading partners and that exporting commodities out of the area was seen as important. It could also be that axes from the three local quarries were so valuable/rare that an exchange imbalance between local axes and other goods was in operation, an imbalance which may have led to some notions of 'credit'.

The axe from the Ffynnondruidion monument, made from either gabbro or quartz dolerite (both coarse-grained igneous rocks), originated from the Isle of Man or Cornwall. However, these isolated finds are rare. It should also be noted that during the Early Bronze Age the famous bluestones (blue-grey dolerite) which form the inner circle at Stonehenge were quarried from three outcrops at Carn Meini, within the heart of the Preselis.

Glossary

Beaker Phase - The name given to a distinctive pottery tradition and subsequent mortuary practice found over the whole of southern Britain. The Beaker tradition is also linked to single-status barrow burials. It was once thought that the Beaker people were invading tribal groups from the Continent. However, this 'invasion' is now considered to be one of ideas rather than of peoples.

Cupmarks - Single and multiple circular gouges cut into stone and interpreted as a form of graffiti used to deface earlier monuments and establish a new identity. They possibly date from the Late Neolithic and extend throughout the Early and Middle Bronze Age.

Cairn - A Bronze Age monument comprising a central cist containing a burial covered by a stone mound.

Cairn Circle - Ring of stone surrounding a cairn (see above).

Cromlech - An antiquarian term for a chambered monument, usually a portal dolmen.

Danubian - refers to an area of Neolithic activity around the River Danube. Main features are longhouses and the distinctive LBK pottery.

Disarticulation - A form of Neolithic burial practice in which limbs were separated from bodies before final interment. It is not clear whether the bones were first defleshed, or whether fresh corpses were dismembered. (see also Excarnation below)

Domus - A concept which is now well established in the social-theory of the Neolithic. It attempts to explain the spread of agri-culture and the domestication (taming) of the landscape. The Domus (or hearth and home)'acts' a familiar reference point within the landscape, creating a sense of belonging.

Earth-fast - A type of megalithic monument identified by Glyn Daniel (1950). The earth-fast tomb consists of a pit covered by a capstone. One end of the covering slab rests on the edge of a pit, the other is supported by an upright stone standing in the pit

Excarnation - The practice of exposing corpses to the elements, perhaps on some kind of specially-constructed platform. North West Coastal American Indians are among peoples known to have practised excarnation.

Forecourt - The public area in front of a tomb delineated by kerbing and horns (see below). This area was apparently reserved for rituals involving ceremonial feasting.

Gallery Grave - Galleries are constructed of large orthostats and roofing slabs and are similar in floor plan to the passage graves (see below). The Gallery is an elongated area lacking side chambers. Some examples have a larger central gallery. The burial tradition is usually considered to be Late Neolithic.

Henge - A circular earthen 'doughnut' structure, usually comparable in size to a large barrow or stone circle. Considered to be Late Neolithic or Early Bronze Age in date, henges are constructed of a simple circular bank and outlying ditch with entrances to an open central space.

Horns (Facade) - These are usually constructed around the facade area of monuments and date from the Late Neolithic. They are found on both trapezoidal and circular monuments and appear to restrict visual access around the facade, as well as to the inside of the passage and the chamber areas (see forecourt).

Hunter/Gatherer/Fisher - This term has been traditionally used to describe small mobile band societies such as the !Kung bushpeople of Southern Africa and earlier Mesolithic groups, prior to settlement and the construction of megalithic chambered tombs. However, the term may refer to a diversity of subsistence strategies relying principally upon naturally-occurring resources rather than cultivated crops and domesticated animals. Such economies may have supported quite complex ranked societies. We would suggest that hunting, fishing and gathering remained an integral part of Neolithic life, especially around the coastal fringes of Wales.

Incognito - This is the merging and blending of a monument within a landscape. Many tombs would have been covered by an earthen or cairn mound, rendering them incognito with the surrounding landscape. Visual access is only possible with knowledge of where and when to look.

Intervisibility - A term used to indicate mutual visibility, usually between corresponding styles of monument. Intervisibilty may indicate a social and political relationship between neighbouring monuments and their people.

Liminal Space - This is a transitional space through which individuals undergoing rites of passage may travel. The most obvious of these is initiation: from boyhood to manhood. But human remains may also past through liminal space on the final journey from life to ancestor status. The long passages evident within some monuments may indicate the path taken during this ritual.

Midden - A term used to describe a rubbish dump, here referring to mounds of shellfish debris which accumulated in some coastal areas during the later Mesolithic as a greater dependence upon marine resources developed.

Monumentality - A visual expression describing the vast imposing presence of a monument. The area of the tomb with maximum monumentality is usually that of the facade area. Here visual impact is greatest.

Passage Grave - A Late Neolithic tomb-type consisting of a chamber set in a round or trapezoidal cairn and approached through a long passage-way. Fine passage graves in Ireland and Anglesey are associated with examples of Megalithic art.

Rank (social stratification) - Rank societies, in which power, prestige and wealth are unequally distributed, are usually distinguished from egalitarianism, in which all are theoretically equal. Changes in burial practice throughout the Neolithic and Early Bronze Age suggest that adult males, who are increasingly singled out for special treatment at death, enjoyed high social rank.

Severn-Cotswold Tradition - This refers to a group of Middle and Late Neolithic tombs located in and around the Severn Valley and on the Cotswolds. Examples are also found in North and South Wales. These tombs are considered to be corporate monuments.

Shaft-Hole Axe - These are usually made from bone or antler and in some cases are decorated. Shaft-hole axes are found throughout southern Scandinavia and the Danubian farming areas suggesting an exchange/ contact economy. The hole would have housed a polished stone or flint axe-head

Stalled Cairn - A tomb-type found in the Orkney Islands which is very similar to the gallery grave design. The main chamber usually runs the length of the cairn and has lateral slabs (stalls) projecting from the chamber wall. These stalls divide the tomb into compartments whilst also supporting the high roofing slabs.

Bibliography

Anonymous account, (1851) 'Account of the fifth annual meeting of the
Cambrian Archaeological Assocoation held at Tenby'.
Archaeologia Cambrensis (2nd Series) 2, 309-333.

Barber, C. & Williams (1989) *The Ancient Stones of Wales*,
Abergavenny. Blorenge Books.

Baring-Gould, S. (1903) 'The Exploration of Clegyr Boia', *Archaeologia
Cambrensis* (6th series) 3, 1-11.

Baring-Gould, S., Burnard, R. and Enys, J.D. (1899) 'Exploration of the
Stone Camp on St David's Head', *Archaeologia Cambrensis* (5th
series) 16, 105-131.

Barker, C.T. (1992) *The Chambered Tombs of South-West Wales: A re-
assessment of the Neolithic burial monuments of Carmarthenshire
and Pembrokeshire*. Oxbow Monograph 14

Barnwell, E.L. (1872) 'Notes on some South Wales Cromlechs',
Archaeologia Cambrensis (4th Series) 3, 81-143.

Barnwell, E.L. (1884) 'On some South Wales Cromlechs', *Archaeologia
Cambrensis* (5th series)1, 129-144.

Beedham, G.E. (1972) *Identification of the British Mollusca*, 40-1.
Hulton.

Bonsall, C. (ed.) (1989) *The Mesolithic in Europe*, Edinburgh University
Press.

Burl, H.A.W. (1976) *The Stone Circles of the British Isles*, Yale
University Press

Bradley, R. (1984) 'Studying Monuments' in R. Bradley and J. Gardiner
(eds.) *Neolithic Studies: A Review of some Current Research*.
B.A.R. British Series 133. 61-66.

Bradley, R. (1992) *Altering the Earth*. The Society of Antiquaries of
Scotland, Monograph Series No.8.

Briggs, S (1982) 'Historical notes on the study of Megalithic and Bronze
age sites and finds from Ceredigion', *Ceredigion* 9, 264-280.

Britnell, W.J. & Savory, H.N. (1984) *Gwernvale and Penywyrlod: Two
Neolithic Long Cairns in the Black Mountains of Brecknock*.
Cambrian Archaeological Monographs No.2

Caseldine, A. (1990) *Environmental Archaeology in Wales*, Cadw Welsh
Historical Monuments & Dept. of Archaeology, St David's
University College, Lampeter.

Castleden, R. (1992) *Neolithic Britain: New Stone Age Sites of England,
Scotland and Wales*, London. Routledge.

Children, G. & Nash, G.H. (1994) *Prehistoric Sites of Herefordshire*,
Logaston Press, Almeley.

Children, G. & Nash, G.H. (1995) 'Sacred Stone, Death and the
Landscape: The Chambered Monuments of South-West Wales'.
New Antiquarian. 22. Gem Publications, 23-28.

Children, G. & Nash, G.H. (1996) *Prehistoric Sites of Monmouthshire*,
Logaston Press, Almeley.

Clough, T.H. & Cummins, W.A. (1988) *Stone Axe Studies Volume 2: The
petrology of prehistoric stone implements from the British Isles.*
CBA Research Report No.67.

Corcorcan, J.X.W.P. (1969) 'The Cotswold-Severn Group', in Powell,
T.G.E. et al. *Megalithic Enquiries in the West of Britain.* 13-104.
Liverpool University Press.

Daniel, G.E. (1950) *The Prehistoric Chambered Tombs of England and
Wales*, Cambridge University Press.

Darvill, T.C. (1982) *The Megalithic Chambered Tombs of the Cotswold-
Severn Region.* Vorda Research Series No.5.

Darvill, T.C. (1983) 'The Neolithic of Wales and the Mid-West of
England: A Systematic Analysis of Social Change through the
Application of Action Theory.' Unpublished Ph.D thesis,
University of Southampton.

Darvill, T.C. (1987) *Prehistoric Britain*, London. Batsford.

Darvill, T.C. (1989) 'The Circulation of Neolithic Stone and Flint Axes:
a case study from Wales and the mid-west of England',
Proceedings of the Prehistoric Society 55, 27-43.

David, A. (1989) 'Some Aspects of the Human Presence in West Wales
during the Mesolithic', in Bonsall, C. (ed.) *The Mesolithic in
Europe*, Edinburgh University Press. 241-253.

Davis, M. (1945) 'Types of Megalithic Monument of the Irish Sea and
North Channel Coastlands: A Study of Distributions', *Antiquity
Journal* 25, 125-144.

Davis, M. (1946) 'The Diffusion and Distribution Pattern of the
Megalithic Monuments of the Irish Sea and the North Channel
Coastlands', *Antiquity Journal* 26, 38-60.

Done Bushell, W. (1911) 'Among the Prescelly Circles'. *Archaeologia
Cambrensis* (6th Series) 11, 287-333.

Dyfed Archaeological Trust (1986) *Archaeology in Dyfed*. Dyfed
Archaeological Trust.

Edmonds, M. (1995) *Stone Tools and Society.* London. Batsford.

Evans, J.G. (1986) *Prehistoric Farmers of Skomer Island: An
Archaeological Guide*. West Wales Trust for Nature Conservation.

Fenton, J. (1848) 'Cromlechs at Llanwnda, Pembrokeshire',
Archaeologia Cambrensis (1st series) 3, 283-5.

Fenton, R. (1810) *A Historical Tour through Pembrokeshire*. London.

Frampton, K. (1992) *Modern architecture: A Critical History*. London. Thames and Hudson. 3rd edition.

Gardner Wilkinson, I. (1871) 'Cromlechs and other remains in Pembrokeshire', *Collectanea Archaeologia* Vol.2, part 2. 219-240.

Grimes, W.F. (1929) 'Pembrokeshire Survey', *Board of Celtic Studies* 5, 277.

Grimes, W.F. (1932) 'Prehistoric Archaeology in Wales since 1925. The Neolithic Period', *Proceedings of the Prehistoric Society of East Anglia* 7, 85-92.

Grimes, W.F. (1936) 'The Megalithic Monuments of Wales', *Proceedings of the Prehistoric Society* 2, 106-139.

Grimes, W.F. (1938) 'Excavations at Meini Gwyr, Carmarthen', *Proceedings of the Prehistoric Society* 4, 324-5.

Grimes, W.F. (1939) 'Bedd y Afanc', *Proceedings of the Prehistoric Society* 5, 258.

Grimes, W.F. (1948) 'Pentre Ifan Burial Chamber, Pembrokeshire', *Archaeologia Cambrensis*, 100. 3-23.

Grimes, W.F. (1984) 'The Neolithic Period', in Savory, H.N. (ed.) *Glamorgan County History Vol 2 - Early Glamorgan*. University of Wales Press: Cardiff. 123-153.

Gronnow, B. (1985) 'Meiendorf and Stellmoor Revisited: An analysis of late Palaeolithic Reindeer exploration', *Acta Archaeologica*, 131-166.

Hemp, W.J. (1927) 'The Capel Garmon Long Cairn'. *Archaeologia Cambrensis,* 82, 1-43

Hodder, I. (1990) *The Domestication of Europe*, Oxford. Blackwell Press.

Hogg, A.H.A. (1974) 'Carn Goch, Carmarthenshire', *Archaeologia Cambrensis* 123, 43-53.

Houlder, C. H. (1978) *Wales: An Archaeological Guide*, London. Faber & Faber.

Houlder, C.H. (1988) 'The Petrological Identification of Stone Implements from Wales', in Clough, T.H. and Cummins, W.A. (eds.) *Stone Axe Studies*, Vol 2. 133-136 & 246-260.

Jones, J. (1847) 'Cromlechs etc. in Pembrokeshire', *Archaeologia Cambrensis* (1st series) 2, 373-4.

Jones, W.B. (1863) 'Double Cromlech on Carn Llidi, in the Parish of St David's, Pembrokeshire', *Archaeologia Cambrensis* (3rd series) 9, 73.

Kinnes, I. (1992) *Non-Megalithic Long Barrows and Allied Structures in the British Neolithic*. British Museum Occasional Paper No.52.

Lacaille, A.D. and Grimes, W.F. (1955) 'The Prehistory of Caldey', *Archaeologia Cambrensis* 104, 85-106.

Lacaille, A.D. and Grimes, W.F. (1961) 'The Prehistory of Caldey, part 2', *Archaeologia Cambrensis* 110, 30-70.

Laws, E. and Owen, H. (1897-1906) *Pembrokeshire Archaeological Survey*.

Leach, A.L. (1932) 'Kichen-Middens on Giltar Point, near Tenby', *Archaeologia Cambrensis* 87, 359-363.

Lee, R. (1968) 'What hunters do for a living, or, how to make out on scarce resources', in Lee, R. and DeVore, I. (eds.), *Man the Hunter*, Chicago. Aldine.

Lee, R. (1979) *The !Kung San: men, women and work in a foraging society*, Cambridge. Cambridge University Press.

Lubbock, J. (1871) *Archaeologia Cambrensis*, 168-172

Lynch, F.M. (1969) 'The Megalithic Tombs of North Wales and The contents of excavated tombs in North Wales' in Powell, T.G.E., et al. *Megalithic Enquires in the West of Britain*. Liverpool University Press. 107-148 and 149-174.

Lynch, F.M. (1972) 'Portal Dolmens of the Nevern Valley', Pembrokeshire, in Lynch, F.M. and Burgess, C. (eds.) *Prehistoric Man in Wales and the West*. 67-84. Adams and Dart.

Lynch, F.M. (1975) 'Excavations at Cerrig Samson Megalithic Tomb, Mathry, Pembrokeshire', *Archaeologia Cambrensis* 124, 15-35.

Lynch, F.M. (1976) 'Towards a Chronology of Megalithic Tombs in Wales' in Boon, G. and Lewis, J. (eds.) *Welsh Antiquity: Essays mainly on Prehistoric Topics*. Presented to Savory, H.N. Cardiff. National Museum of Wales. 63-79.

Lynch, F.M. (1984) 'The Neolithic Pottery. Part 2. Discussion', in Britnell, W.J. & Savory, H.N. 1984. 106-110.

Lynch, F.M. & Burgess, C. (eds.) (1972) *Prehistoric Man in Wales and the West*, Bath. Adams and Dart.

Mack, J. (1986) *Madagascar: Land of the Ancestors*. London. British Museum Press

Massey, D. (1994) *Space, Place and Gender*, Cambridge. Polity Press.

Masters, L. (1981) 'Chambered Tombs and Non-Megalithic Barrows in Britain', in *Antiquity and Man; Essays in Honour of Glyn Daniel*, Evans, J.D. et al., Thames & Hudson, 1981, 161-176.

Matthews, A.W. (1926) 'Marros: Chamber Cairn on Morfa Bycham, 1926', *Transactions of Carmarthen Antiquarian Society* 20, 82.

Morris, R.W.B. (1989) 'The Prehistoric Rock Art of Great Britain; A survey of all Sites bearing Motifs more Complex than Simple Cupmarks', *Proceedings of the Prehistoric Society* 55, 48-88.

Murphy, K. (1986) 'Marros Mountain, Eglwys Cummin', *Archaeology in Wales* 25, 36.

Nash, G.H. (1998) *Status, Exchange and Mobility: Mesolithic portable art of Southern Scandinavia*, Oxford. BAR International Series No.5710.

O'Kelly, M.J. (1981) 'The Megalithic Tombs of Ireland', in *Antiquity and Man; Essays in Honour of Glyn Daniel*, Evans, J.D. et al., Thames & Hudson, 1981, 177-190.

Piggott, S. (1954) *The Neolithic Cultures of the British Isles*, Cambridge. Cambridge University Press.

Pitts, M. (1980) *Later Stone Implements*. Shire Archaeology Series No. 14.

Powell, T.G.E. (1973) 'Excavation of the Megalithic Chambered Cairn at Dyffryn Ardudwy, Merioneth, Wales', *Archaeologia* 104, 1-50.

Powell, T.G.E., Corcoran, J.X.W.P., Lynch, F. & Scott, J.G. (1969) *Megalithic Enquiries in the West of Britain*, Liverpool University Press.

RCAM, (1917) *An Inventory of the Ancient Monuments in Wales and Monmouthshire V. Carmarthenshire* HMSO.

RCAM, (1925) *An Inventory of the Ancient Monuments in Wales and Monmouthshire VII. County of Pembroke* HMSO.

Reed, A.W. (1965) *Aboriginal Fables and Legendary Tales*, (self-published)

Rees, S. (1981) *The Archaeology of Dyfed*. Cadw, Cardiff.

Rees, T. (1815) *A Topographical and Historical Description of South Wales*, London. Sherwood, Neely and Jones.

Renfrew, C. (1979) *Investigations in Orkney*, London. Society of Antiquaries.

Savory, H.N. (1953) 'Twlc y filiast cromlech', *Bulletin of the Board of Celtic Studies* 15, (part 3), 225-228.

Savory, H.N. (1956) 'The Excavation of Twlc y filiast cromlech, Llangynog', *Bulletin of the Board of Celtic Studies* 16, (part 4), 300-308.

Savory, H.N. (1980) 'The Neolithic in Wales', in J.A.Taylor (ed.) *Culture and Environment in Prehistoric Wales*. British Archaeological Report No.76: Oxford. 207-232.

Simpson, C. (1953) *Plumes and Arrows: Inside New Guinea,* Sydney. Angus &Robertson.

Stanford, S.C. (1991) *The Archaeology of the Welsh Marches* (2nd Edition). Luston. Privately published.

Swanton, J.R. (1946) 'The Indians of the south-western United States. Smithsonian Institution'. *Bureau of American Ethnography*. Bulletin 137

Taylor, J.A. (1980) 'Culture and Environment' in *Prehistoric Wales*, Oxford, BAR British series 76

Thomas, J. (1990) *Rethinking the Neolithic*, Cambridge. Cambridge University Press.

Thomas, J. (1993) 'The politics of vision and the archaeologies of landscape', in Bender, B. (ed.) *Landscape, Politics and Perspectives*. Berg.

Thorpe, I.J. (1984) 'Ritual Power and Ideology: A Reconstruction of Earlier Neolithic Rituals in Wessex' in Bradley, R. and Gardiner, J. (eds.) *Neolithic Studies: A Review of some Current Research*. B.A.R. British Series 133. 41-60.

Tilley, C. (1991) *Material Culture and Text: The Art of Ambiguity*. London. Routledge.

Tilley, C. (1993) 'The Politics of Man and the Archaeology of Landscape' in Bender, B. (ed.) *Landscape, Politics and Perspectives*. Berg.

Tilley, C. (1994) *A Phenomenology of Landscape: Paths, Places and Monuments*, London. Berg.

Turnbull, C.M. (1962) *The Forest People*, Touchstone Press

Ward, J. (1918) 'Some prehistoric sepulchral remains near Pendine, Carmarthenshire'. *Archaeologia Cambrensis* 18, 6th Series, 35-79

Ward, A.H. (1976) 'The Cairns on Mynydd Llangyndeyrn: A Focal point of the Early Bronze Age in South-East Dyfed', *The Carmarthenshire Antiquary* 12, 3-21.

Ward, P.A., Williams, G.H., Marshall, E.C. & Drake, I.M. (1987) 'The Glandy Cross Complex', *Archaeology in Wales* 27, 9-13.

Williams, A. (1953) 'Clegyr Boia, St David's, Pembrokeshire: Excavations in 1943', *Archaeologia Cambrensis* 102, 20-47.

Williams, G. (1984) 'A Henge Monument at Ffynnon Newydd, Nantgaredig', *Bulletin of the Board of Celtic Studies* 31, 177-190.

Worsley, P. (1967) 'Groote Eylandt Totemism and Le Totemisme aujourd'hui' in Leach (ed.) *The Structural Study of Myth and Totemism*, 141-160. Tavistock.

Wymer, J.J. (1977) *Gazetteer of Mesolithic sites in England and Wales*, C.B.A. (Council for British Archaeology), Research Report No.22.

Zvelebil, M. (ed.) (1986) *Hunters in Transition: Mesolithic Societies of temperate Eurasia and their Transition to Farming*, Cambridge. Cambridge University Press.

Index

Entries in italic indicate the main, separate site entry for the monument.

Also from Logaston Press

The Story of the Milford Haven Waterway
The Good Times and the Bad Times
by Sybil Edwards

This book focusses on how the Milford Haven waterway has shaped and developed the fortunes of the settlements along its shores, from the arrival of early man through to the present day.

Tracing the arrival of our prehistoric ancestors, the story develops with the arrival of the Romans. Then followed the Dark Ages from which emerged the multitude of Welsh kingdoms that often fought with one another. Into this feuding mix arrived the Normans, Flemings and English. The Landsker, a line of castles across the peninsula, soon created 'Little England beyond Wales'. Growing trade with Ireland led initially Pembroke and then Haverfordwest (as well as Tenby) to develop into thriving ports, safeguarded by their own castles. Along the shores a multitude of small sailing craft were built.

The waterway with all its creeks and inlets was also a haven for smugglers and pirates, often aided and abetted by those with some responsibility to control their activity. Even so, sea-borne trade in agricultural produce—initially corn, wood, salt, wine and ale—quickened when local mines started producing quality anthracite, and with the establishment of lime kilns. Ships grew in size and Pembroke Dock beacme a naval dockyard, whilst Milford became the main fishing port, supported by Neyland. Various schemes for the fortification of the waterway saw a flurry of forts, towers and barracks, their design often rapidly overtaken by changes in military technology. Pembroke Dock thrived for over 100 years before it fell from grace, becoming at first a graveyard for boats being scrapped, then a flying boat base around the time of the Second World War.

Since then the waters have served the need of oil supply, sharing the associated dangers of such activity, and now looks to more leisure use.

£12.95 with over 100 photos, plans and illustrations.